State Secrecy and Democracy

In the wake of controversial disclosures of classified government information by WikiLeaks and Edward Snowden, questions about the democratic status of secret uses of political power are rarely far from the headlines. Despite an increase in initiatives aimed at enhancing government transparency – such as freedom of information or sunshine laws – secrecy persists in both the foreign and domestic policy of democratic states, in the form of classified intelligence programs, espionage, secret military operations, diplomatic discretion, closed-door political bargaining, and bureaucratic opacity.

This book explores whether the state's claim to restrict access to information can be justified. Dorota Mokrosinska answers this question with a qualified "yes," arguing that secrecy in exercising executive and legislative power can be seen as a legitimate exercise of democratic authority rather than as its justified suspension.

Past and recent examples of state secrecy are used throughout the book, including the Manhattan Project, decision-making leading to the Iraq War, the extraordinary renditions programs and secret detention sites in Eastern Europe, collaboration between international secret services, and the WikiLeaks and Snowden disclosures.

State Secrecy and Democracy: A Philosophical Inquiry is essential reading for those in political philosophy, ethics, politics, international relations and security studies, and law.

Dorota Mokrosinska is Associate Professor at the Institute for Philosophy, Leiden University, the Netherlands. She is the author of *Rethinking Political Obligation: Moral Principles, Communal Ties, Citizenship* (2012), co-editor (with B. Roessler) of *Social Dimensions of Privacy: Interdisciplinary Perspectives* (2015), and *Secrecy and Transparency in European Democracies: Contested Trade-Offs* (Routledge, 2020).

Routledge Focus on Philosophy

Routledge Focus on Philosophy is an exciting and innovative new series, capturing and disseminating some of the best and most exciting new research in philosophy in short book form. Peer reviewed and at a maximum of fifty thousand words shorter than the typical research monograph, *Routledge Focus on Philosophy* titles are available in both ebook and print on demand format. Tackling big topics in a digestible format the series opens up important philosophical research for a wider audience, and as such is invaluable reading for the scholar, researcher and student seeking to keep their finger on the pulse of the discipline. The series also reflects the growing interdisciplinarity within philosophy and will be of interest to those in related disciplines across the humanities and social sciences.

Moral Choices for Our Future Selves
An Empirical Theory of Prudential Perception and a Moral Theory of Prudence
Eleonora Viganò

Moralistics and Psychomoralistics
A Unified Cognitive Science of Moral Intuition
Graham Wood

Idealism after Existentialism
Encounters in Philosophy of Religion
N.N. Trakakis

State Secrecy and Democracy
A Philosophical Inquiry
Dorota Mokrosinska

For more information about this series, please visit: www.routledge.com/Routledge-Focus-on-Philosophy/book-series/RFP

State Secrecy and Democracy

A Philosophical Inquiry

Dorota Mokrosinska

Routledge
Taylor & Francis Group
LONDON AND NEW YORK

First published 2024
by Routledge
4 Park Square, Milton Park, Abingdon, Oxon OX14 4RN

and by Routledge
605 Third Avenue, New York, NY 10158

Routledge is an imprint of the Taylor & Francis Group, an informa business

British Library Cataloguing-in-Publication Data
A catalogue record for this book is available from the British Library

Library of Congress Cataloging-in-Publication Data
Names: Mokrosinska, Dorota, author.
Title: State secrecy and democracy : a philosophical inquiry / Dorota Mokrosinska.
Description: Abingdon, Oxon ; New York, NY : Routledge, 2024. | Series: Routledge focus on philosophy | Includes bibliographical references and index.
Identifiers: LCCN 2023036956 (print) | LCCN 2023036957 (ebook) | ISBN 9780367539238 (hardback) | ISBN 9780367539276 (paperback) | ISBN 9781003083733 (ebook)
Subjects: LCSH: Executive privilege (Government information) | Democracy.
Classification: LCC JK468.S4 M59 2024 (print) | LCC JK468.S4 (ebook) | DDC 352.23/5—dc23/eng/20230822
LC record available at https://lccn.loc.gov/2023036956
LC ebook record available at https://lccn.loc.gov/2023036957

ISBN: 978-0-367-53923-8 (hbk)
ISBN: 978-0-367-53927-6 (pbk)
ISBN: 978-1-003-08373-3 (ebk)

DOI: 10.4324/9781003083733

Typeset in Times New Roman
by Apex CoVantage, LLC

Contents

Acknowledgement

This book is part of the research project "Democratic Secrecy: A Philosophical Study of the Role of Secrecy in Democratic Governance," which has received funding from the European Research Council under the European Union's Horizon 2020 research and innovation program (DEMSEC GA 639021).

1 Introduction

This book explores the democratic status of government secrecy. The project is revisionary, if not heretical. In the political rhetoric of modern democracies, as Pierre Rosanvallon observes, transparency has risen to the status of "the new democratic ideal."[1] Secrecy, as the opposite of transparency, has been denounced as undemocratic.

Proceeding under the presumption in favor of transparency, democratic theory has paid little systematic attention to the normative status of secrecy in governance.[2] Insofar as contemporary scholarship engages with the topic, it is in contexts of abuses of secrecy in political practice and measures to combat these abuses.[3]

The only systematic attention to state secrecy was in the medieval doctrine of "mysteries of the state" and the early-modern doctrine of "arcana imperii."[4] These doctrines incorporated secrecy into an arsenal of legitimate techniques for the execution, maintenance, and expansion of political power. With the exception of political realists and the "reasons of state" approach to politics,[5] these theories have not found followers in modern political thought.

The modern eschewal of secrecy in governance, as Eva Horn observes, coincides with the emergence of the social contract tradition: when citizens authorize political power, their exclusion from knowledge about the government's activities and decisions is hard to accept.[6] As democratic ideas have come to dominate contemporary political thought, the presumption in favor of publicity, and against secrecy, has been reinforced. Transparency has come to be cherished as a synonym for clarity, coherence, and sincerity in the handling of public affairs and the condition of democratic legitimacy: it ensures that citizens have the information they need to participate as equals in collective decision-making, and it guarantees citizens' control over office holders and institutions. From this perspective, classified government information, secret diplomacy, and closed-door political bargaining appear troubling because they exclude citizens from political participation and inhibit the mechanisms of governments' democratic accountability.

Without denying the relevance of transparency, two factors motivate paying more systematic attention to secrecy in democratic governance. The first is

DOI: 10.4324/9781003083733-1

the persistence of secrecy in democratic politics. Despite democratic rhetoric and an increase in initiatives aimed at enhancing legal and political transparency, such as freedom of information or sunshine laws, the culture of secrecy entrenched in political institutions has proved hard to uproot.[7] The realm of state secrecy persists in both the foreign and domestic policy of democratic states, taking the form of classified intelligence programs, espionage, secret military operations, diplomatic discretion, closed-door political bargaining, and bureaucratic opacity. Research on how political institutions respond to transparency-enhancing provisions demonstrates that governmental institutions make compensatory adjustments that render transparency-enhancing measures ineffective. Strategies range from thwarting disclosure requests to the development of media-spin politics and the destruction of information records.[8] If transparency, as Mark Fenster puts it, provides such "a remarkable array of benefits that no right-thinking politician, administrator, policy wonk, or academic could be against it,"[9] how come it is resisted?

The second factor is a recent wave of research, which indicates the drawbacks of transparency. These include harm to a state's interests when sensitive information, for example, military or intelligence, is at stake, and in international tensions over revelations of diplomatic confidences. A number of policy-oriented studies demonstrate that transparency-overload discourages innovative behavior and triggers defensive information management, proceduralism, and rule-obsession. Scholars point out that rigorous transparency policies, by allowing for constant observation and surveillance, accounting, auditing, and oversight, lead to decision-making that is governed more by fear and avoidance of the appearance of wrongdoing than appropriate risk taking in response to social and political challenges. As administrators are being scrutinized more frequently and thoroughly, they get better at meeting the requirements posed by their accountability forums, while not necessarily performing better in terms of effective policy-making.[10] Drawbacks of transparency aside, a concern has been voiced about its feasibility. Fenster argues that the sheer organizational complexity of the state and the fact that its administrative apparatus is dispersed over a large number of agencies with significant decision-making autonomy and spread over large geographical territories make it impossible to develop and implement the technocratic tools that would make the state fully open.[11]

By pointing to diminishing returns on transparency, these critical transparency studies offer reasons explaining the resistance to transparency. If there are reasons for resisting full transparency, are they, at the same time, reasons for endorsing a degree of secrecy in democratic governance? This will not follow if ruling by secret policies and processes does not fall within the remit of the authority democratic states exercise.

I focus on representative democracy, the most prevalent form of democratic governance. I adopt standard contemporary usage of this term, which refers to states in which citizens, exercising an equal right to vote, choose their representatives, who then have the right to make laws and policies on citizens' behalf and in the light of their interests. Authorized to take decisions and make policy, representatives owe citizens an account of how they advance their interests. Besides accountability, democratic representation involves responsiveness and communication between representatives and citizens in a way that ensures that citizens remain co-authors of laws and policies. In order to ensure such responsiveness and communication, democracies, next to offering protections to the equal right to vote and running for office, must have effective protections of political, civil, and personal freedoms such as freedom of speech and association or a right to privacy.

Decisions taken by representatives are meant to be authoritative, that is, binding on all citizens. Without committing to any specific theory of democratic authority, the question I explore in this book is: does the authority democratic states hold warrant their resort to secrecy? The book answers this question with a qualified yes.

I start off with a critical examination of the political myth of transparency. Chapter 2 introduces a distinction between the consequentialist and non-consequentialist defenses of transparency. The former defends transparency in terms of the benefits it is believed to bring about. The latter presents transparency as valuable for its own sake rather than in virtue of its beneficial consequences: transparency verifies the justice of a state's actions and/or testifies to the "people's right to know." The chapter concludes that both consequentialist and non-consequentialist defenses of transparency must be committed to making room for secrecy in governance and, thus, that the political imperative of transparency is less categorical than its consequentialist and non-consequentialist proponents profess.

If the political imperative of transparency is less categorical than assumed, does this mean that secrecy in governance can be a legitimate exercise of democratic authority?

Political authority exercised by democratic states is the moral and legal power, or right, to rule by imposing its laws and orders, subject to a set of limiting conditions. If a state's resort to secrecy is to be an exercise of democratic authority, it must be seen as a manifestation of that power and hedged by a similar set of limiting conditions. The following chapters consider whether state secrecy can be framed in these terms.

Chapter 3 explores the dominant defense of state secrecy, often invoked by executive actors. By this argument, secrecy is a legitimate exercise of democratic authority if it is a necessary measure called for in circumstances in which basic interests of the state are at stake, for instance, national security and/or the effectiveness of government action. Arguments defending state secrecy by appealing to its necessity, I argue, follow the logic of the raison d'état tradition and fail to escape its anti-democratic implications. In particular, an appeal to necessity fails to confer political and/or legal authority on the state's resort to secrecy because necessity escapes normative codification in both the moral and legal domains ("necessity knows no law"). In this it opens the door to unconstrained power. Drawing a distinction between legitimacy and vindication, I claim, however, that even though an appeal to necessity does not suffice to legitimate government secrecy, it may vindicate it.

Chapter 4 addresses an argument that defends the state's claim to restrict access as a matter of state rights *viz.* its right to privacy. What brings this argument close to the necessity argument is the idea that privacy is a "functional necessity," as the by-now-classic privacy scholar Alan Westin put it.[12] By this view, first articulated in classic liberal privacy scholarship in the 1970s and revived in the aftermath of the WikiLeaks and Snowden disclosures, states, just like individuals, have a right to privacy: "executive privacy" and "legislative privacy" are a shield protecting the "organizational autonomy" of the state in the same way in which individual privacy is seen as a shield protecting individual autonomy.[13] The main objection to this view is that rights pertain to individuals only: groups, including states, cannot exercise rights, privacy, or otherwise. In response, I claim that rights to group privacy may be defended and that we may grant privacy to, for example, private clubs, institutions, business corporations, or juries. However, I argue that governments and parliaments are not the kind of groups that may exercise a right to privacy against citizens. This is because granting the state a right to privacy is conceptually inconsistent with its democratic accountability, which is a necessary (though not sufficient) element of democratic authority.

Chapters 5 and 6 develop a novel approach to secrecy in democratic governance and constitute this book's main contribution to the existing scholarship. Chapter 5, focusing on executive power, develops an alternative defense of state secrecy in democratic governance. Drawing on the formal features of political authority exercised by democratic states, it argues that the political authority democratic governments exercise actually involves a right to resort to secrecy, this right being a special case of the right to rule in the content-independent way with which democratic states are vested. This argument shifts the normative grounds for secrecy from reasons that the actors exercising political authority might entertain when classifying government information, such as the "functional necessity" of withholding information, to the nature of the power they hold. This defense of state secrecy does what the necessity- and privacy-based arguments set out to do but fail: it extends political authority to policies and processes that the executive deems necessary to classify. Yet it does this not in virtue of their necessity but in virtue of the right to rule that democratic governments hold. Unlike the necessity- and privacy-based arguments, this defense of state secrecy comes with in-built limits upon the state's resort to secrecy and a demand that the secrecy afforded to the state be rendered accountable. Only if these conditions are satisfied does the government authority to resort to secrecy take normative effect.

While this argument offers a case in favor of secrecy, it does not deny the value of transparency for democratic governance. For example, it does not claim that transparency measures – such as freedom of information laws (FOIA) – should be abandoned. Rather, it offers an argument defending the exemption of a certain class of political decisions and processes from disclosure, and it does this in terms of democratic authority rather than in terms of raison d'état, necessity or the state's right to privacy.

Chapter 6 moves from secrecy in exercising executive power to legislative power. Legislative assemblies exercise content-independent political authority. As per the argument developed in the previous chapter, their resort to secrecy is authoritative provided it meets a set of limiting conditions. Rather than rehearsing the argument to this effect, this chapter contributes to the reflection on the conditions under which the legislative assembly's authority to resort to secrecy can take normative effect. Democracy scholars have acknowledged that publicity can stymie legislative deliberation thus inhibiting the legislative capacity to act; when this is the case, legislative deliberation may be moved behind closed doors. The impact of publicity on legislative voting has received no systematic attention in normative democratic theory.[14] This chapter contributes to this unexplored tack of the debate in the discussion of secrecy and transparency in democratic governance. Following recent developments in democratic theory, which present voting and deliberation as complementary rather than competing models for democratic decision-making, it argues that the same reasons that support moving parliamentary deliberations behind closed doors may also support moving parliamentary voting behind closed doors.

Notes

1 Rosanvallon 2008, 258.
2 Rather than to secrecy on the part of government agents, scholars have paid more attention to the question of secrecy on the part of citizens. This discussion revolves around the question of the secret versus open ballot in democratic elections. For arguments in favor of the secret ballot, see Lever 2007; Johnson and Orr 2020. For arguments in favor of the open ballot, see Brennan and Pettit 1990; Engelen and Nys 2013.
3 For example, Sagar 2007, 2013; Colaresi 2014. Exceptions are Thompson 1999; Kogelmann 2021.
4 Machiavelli 1988/1532; Botero 2017/1589.
5 Meinecke 1998; Schmitt (2014).
6 Horn 2011, 104, 114.
7 Roberts 2006(b); Curtin 2011; Sagar 2013; Mokrosinska 2020(b).
8 Roberts 2006(b), 110–112; Murray 2005, 201.
9 Fenster 2006, 888–889.
10 Anechiarico and Jacobs 1996; Bovens 2010, 958.
11 Fenster 2010.
12 Westin 1967, 49.
13 Westin 1967, 49; Bloustein 1977, 257.
14 Kogelmann 2021 is an exception. For empirical literature on the impact of transparency on parliamentary voting, see, for example, Naurin 2006.

2 Government transparency

Grounds and limits

2.1 Introduction

Transparency has captured our political imagination rising to the status of, as Pierre Rosanvallon observed, the "paramount virtue" of modern democratic politics.[1] At nearly every level of governance, reforms that seek greater transparency are increasingly on the agendas of governments, international organizations, and civil society. When in 2009 the newly elected President Barack Obama signed the *Memorandum on Transparency and Open Government*, he pledged to work toward "an unprecedented level of openness in Government [which] will strengthen our democracy and promote efficiency and effectiveness in Government."[2] Similar mission statements have been issued by international bodies, for example, the "European Transparency Initiative" of the EU Commission.[3] Transparency has been applauded by the OECD as one of the "pillars for democracy, trust and progress"[4] and hailed by the World Bank for improving the economic performance and morals of the markets. Watchdog organizations and NGOs such as Transparency International champion transparency as a powerful anti-corruption tool.

Defined as the availability of government information that allows citizens to monitor the workings and performance of government,[5] transparency is presented as a key to more democratic and effective governance: it promises to empower citizens to influence political decision-making processes, hold office holders accountable, reduce public corruption, and foster greater trust in government. Framed in this "transformative narrative,"[6] transparency is contrasted with secrecy, which has been seen as a symbol of arbitrary and tyrannical power and associated with conspiracy and corruption. In this spirit, Jackie Davis, editor of *European Voice*, a Brussels-based weekly newspaper devoted to coverage of EU affairs, pleaded for "lifting the veil of secrecy" as a cure for EU institutions' democratic deficits: "The veil of secrecy does nobody any good, it merely perpetuates the image of the EU as a mysterious, remote and undemocratic body . . . taking decisions . . . without proper consultation and public debate."[7]

This chapter critically examines the political myth of transparency. The most influential arguments raised in its favor are of a consequentialist character and defend transparency in terms of the benefits it is believed to bring

DOI: 10.4324/9781003083733-2

about. Sections 2.2 and 2.3 review these arguments in light of a rapidly growing body of empirical research on the impact of transparency on governance. Section 2.4 turns to non-consequentialist arguments, which present transparency as valuable for its own sake rather than in virtue of its beneficial consequences. These arguments often feature in political and legal transparency rhetoric presenting transparency as a token of justice (Section 2.4.1) or as a matter of human or civil rights (Section 2.4.2). Unlike the consequentialist arguments, non-consequentialist arguments in favor of transparency have not been systematically examined. Aiming to give them a proper place on the map of transparency studies, I pay special attention to the argument linking transparency to the rights discourse. Having critically examined the consequentialist and non-consequentialist arguments, I conclude in Section 2.5 that both consequentialist and non-consequentialist defenses of transparency, contrary to what their proponents profess, must be committed to making room for secrecy in governance.

2.2 The consequentialist arguments for transparency

Transparency reforms are often framed in terms of their beneficial effects on the quality of governance. Forerunners of this consequentialist argument are Jeremy Bentham and John Stuart Mill. Strictly speaking, Bentham and Mill did not defend "transparency" but "publicity" in public affairs; the term "transparency" entered public discourse only in the late 20th century. However, most contemporary authors treat these terms as synonymous, and the contemporary enchantment with transparency is similar to what made the 18th- and 19th-century philosophers defend publicity as a principle governing public affairs.[8] Next, I examine the most influential consequentialist arguments for transparency and show their problematic aspects.

2.2.1 "The eye of the public makes the statesman virtuous"

Bentham, the author of the quote opening this section,[9] saw publicity as a means of improving the moral quality of political power.[10] He argued that the creation and maintenance of public records and the opening, wherever possible, of state proceedings to public observers would subject office holders to judgments and sanctions of the people. Such exposure to the "tribunal of public opinion" would deter misconduct of office holders, diminish temptation of corruption, and foster integrity. In line with Bentham, as Jenny de Fine Licht observes, contemporary transparency advocates defend greater openness in public affairs in terms of the increased opportunities it would create for citizens to discipline office holders by subjecting them to public control. Since the public has the ultimate power to remove them from office, the risk of the exposure of misconduct to public criticism is believed to give office holders a strong incentive to look credible and trustworthy in the eyes of the audience and avoid inefficiency, neglect, or corruption.[11] The logic is simple: the more closely they are watched, the better they behave.

Empirical findings on the moralizing effect of transparency are not conclusive. For one, it is not clear whether more transparency translates into more control; for another, it is unclear whether more control implies more discipline. As research demonstrates, transparency-enhancing provisions may actually undercut control mechanisms by triggering defensive information management. This may range from public officials committing less to paper, to failing to keep appropriate records, to the destruction of information records, and to the development of media-spin politics.[12] Examples from actual political practice abound: in 2012, the UK government refused to grant a FOIA request to release the minutes of its March 2003 meetings when it took the decision to go to war in Iraq. In the Statement of Reasons supporting this decision, it asserted that transparency could prompt office holders to hold such discussions "off the record," thereby reducing the opportunity for public control.[13] Another remarkable example of the lack of controlling effect of transparency-enhancing measures is the way in which the Dutch Ministry of Health, Welfare and Sport dealt with a FOIA request to share information about the controversial face mask deal at the start of the coronavirus pandemic in 2020. Despite a court order backing the FOIA request, the Ministry chose to pay a penalty over releasing the information.[14]

Even in cases in which transparency does serve as a control mechanism, this does not automatically imply that it has any disciplining impact. Instead of eliminating misconduct, transparency-induced control may simply shift it from one realm to another. For example, in her analysis of human rights practices in 145 countries from 1975 to 2000, Emilie Hafner-Burton demonstrates that governments publicly criticized for human rights violations reduced some of them but continued or even intensified others.[15] Or, as Monika Bauhr and Marcia Grimes observe, transparency may entrench institutional misconduct. This is the case if transparency reveals institutional wrongdoing, but mechanisms of accountability are not in place or are perceived as inadequate. Powerlessness in the face of institutional wrongdoing triggers resigned acceptance of it as the most efficient way to "get things done."[16] This explains why in highly corrupt countries, transparency fails to combat but actually preserves corruption.[17]

I conclude that in light of empirical research, the argument defending transparency in terms of its moralizing impact on politics is less compelling than transparency advocates profess.

2.2.2 Public trust

As proclaimed in Obama's "Memorandum on Transparency and Open Government," one of the prominent goals his administration meant to achieve by creating openness in government was to "to ensure public trust."[18] Like

Obama's Memorandum, much political transparency rhetoric emphasizes its positive impact on the degree of citizens' trust in public institutions and office holders.[19] Contemporary scholarship considers public trust as a measure of the perceived legitimacy of the political order.[20] From this perspective, the more transparent the system, the more legitimate it is in people's eyes and the more public allegiance and support it enjoys.

Bentham linked the impact of publicity on public trust to the improved quality of governance that publicity would bring about. The virtuousness of office holders, induced by publicity, he expected, would enhance "the confidence of the people."[21] According to contemporary scholars, transparency of government processes increases public perceptions of their legitimacy because it enhances people's understanding of the "how and why" of political decisions. Drawing on deliberative democracy scholarship,[22] transparency advocates argue that an increased understanding of the complexities of political decision-making and of the trade-offs between the competing interests they involve induces legitimacy beliefs on the part of citizens who are subject to them.

Neither the claim that transparency leads to better understanding of government processes nor the claim that better understanding of government processes fosters public perceptions of their legitimacy has straightforward empirical support. In an overview of recent research addressing the correlation between trust and transparency, Qiushi Wang and Zhen Guan report "a considerable disparity in theoretical arguments and empirical findings."[23]

Empirical studies register no direct correlation between enhanced transparency and improved citizens' understanding of government. Instead, they demonstrate that the impact of transparency on public knowledge is strongly mediated by external factors. Depending on their presence or absence, the impact of transparency on public understanding may be positive or negative.

One important factor mediating the effect of government transparency on public knowledge of government is citizens' pre-existing interest in government. In a UK-based study on the effect of FOI legislation, Ben Worthy found that making information available to citizens who are not interested in it has no desired effect. As one of his government official interviewees put it, "[I]f people don't care, you are not going to make them care" by providing them with more information.[24] The knowledge-enhancing effect of transparency obtains only with regard to a select group of citizens, such as FOI requesters, who are already interested in government, engaged in political agenda-setting, policy deliberation, and decision-making. However, as we will see later, even regarding this group, the increase of knowledge of government need not translate into perceiving it as more trustworthy.

Another factor affecting the impact of transparency on public knowledge is the framing of government information that becomes available. Unless contextualized, edited, and presented in ways that make it possible for citizens to comprehend their relevance, information disclosures may lead to confusion rather than to increased understanding.[25] To illustrate this effect, Alasdair Roberts points to the lack of public reaction to the massive release of US military documents by WikiLeaks in 2008. The documents described techniques to infiltrate and stoke an insurgency to overthrow a foreign government, commit sabotage, and economic and financial warfare. Contrary to WikiLeaks' expectations, no public response followed. As Assange's collaborator admitted, "[N]o one cared because the subject matter was too complex."[26]

Just as no direct correlation between transparency and enhanced public knowledge of government has been registered, so also no direct correlation between enhanced public knowledge and public trust has been found.[27] Again, the effect of increased public knowledge of government processes on public trust is dependent on external factors and may turn positive as well as negative. For example, Jenny de Fine Licht observes that depending on the content of the disclosed information, transparency may *decrease* the perceived legitimacy of political systems precisely because of the *increased* understanding it provides.[28] For instance, increased knowledge may focus people's attention on small errors or flaws. A focus on minor mistakes may lead to frame government as incompetent or unresponsive to the needs of citizens and result in a decrease of trust.[29] Of relevance here is the framing of government disclosures in the media, which often involves controversy and negative bias. Indeed, Worthy argues that the negativity bias is responsible for the fact that trust in political institutions has not increased in the UK despite the adoption of freedom of information laws.[30] Alasdair Roberts makes similar observations regarding Canada and the United States.[31]

Transparency advocates may downplay the significance of these empirical findings, arguing that they overlook the true essence of the argument, which emphasizes positive rather than negative transparency. When accurately interpreted, the argument asserts that transparency increases people's trust when government performs well and is seen to perform well as compared to when it performs well but is not seen to be doing so. Even if formulated in this way, however, the argument has no conclusive empirical support. Albert Meijer, Paul 't Hart, and Ben Worthy report that people "punish" poor-performing authorities but do not reward well-performing ones.[32] Likewise, Wang and Guan found that "people tend to be more sensitive to negative transparency than to positive transparency, making transparency a highly ineffective tool to improve citizens' trust."[33]

In conclusion, the impact of transparency on public trust and perceptions of government legitimacy is less pronounced than transparency advocates proclaim. Trust and public perceptions of legitimacy of government are primarily anchored in factors other than transparency; transparency plays only a subordinate role in fostering them, if at all.

2.2.3 Informed governance

Transparency is cherished as a tool for more informed governance. According to one version of this argument, initially formulated by Bentham, this effect is predicated in transparency's educational impact. On this view, disclosing government decisions would enable citizens to form more informed political opinions and make better electoral choices. More informed public opinion, in turn, would enable governors to make better policy decisions by drawing on citizens' feedback and expertise. Bentham's argument resonates with contemporary arguments for open government. According to Obama's "Memorandum," transparency will enhance citizens' political engagement by offering them "increased opportunities to participate in policy-making and to provide their Government with the benefits of their collective expertise and information," which, in turn, will "enhance the Government's effectiveness and improve the quality of its decisions."[34]

The argument assumes that citizens make use of access to government information. Empirical research sheds doubt on the validity of this assumption. It has been shown that lack of resources in terms of time and expertise frustrates people's capacity to process government information. According to other findings, citizens often adopt the attitude of "rational ignorance" refusing to invest in information-seeking if the cost of acquiring information exceeds the potential benefit they expected it would provide.[35] These findings explain the low rate of FOIA requests for government information submitted by average citizens. Worthy's research demonstrates that, as a general rule, the users of FOIA legislation comprise a mixture of businesses, NGOs, and journalists, with average citizens responsible for fewer than 1 in 1,000 requests.[36] Given that citizens generally do not make use of transparency-enhancing measures, the beneficial impact these measures have on citizens' political expertise may be weaker than transparency advocates presuppose.

According to another version of the argument, transparency would lead to more informed governance because of its beneficial impact on the quality of political deliberation and decision-making. Historically, the argument has its source in Mill's "Considerations on Representative Government."[37] Mill argued that exposure to the public view would weed out private biases and discourage sloppy reasoning on the part of decision-makers: in anticipation of being called to account for what they say, they would make sure to formulate their positions in a way that does not undermine their credibility.[38]

In contemporary scholarship, Mill's argument has been reinvigorated by deliberative democrats. Deliberative democrats link political deliberation to the process of public justification, which they see as a condition of legitimacy of political decisions in pluralist and diverse societies.[39] Public justification requires that whenever we decide what laws and policies to adopt, we must appeal to public reasons *viz*. reasons that those subjected to such laws and policies can accept. Transparency is believed to facilitate the use of public *reason* because it enhances the epistemic dimension of reasoning through which office holders articulate their positions: it creates the pressure to collect and examine all facts relevant to the issue to hand, to consider alternative viewpoints, and to formulate their argument with due care.[40] Transparency is believed to facilitate the use of *public* reason because it stimulates the use of reasons that appeals to general rather than private interests.[41] In her discussion of the impact of publicity on political deliberations, Simone Chambers summarized this position thus:

> The logic here is that publicly arguing for a policy on the grounds, say, that it makes you better off is not a *public* reason and will not get very far within a modern liberal democratic public sphere. The democratic dynamic makes obviously selfish, narrow or sectarian defenses of public policy . . . difficult to pursue in public.[42]

Some theorists like John Dryzek and Jon Elster explain this mechanism in terms of individual psychology and cognitive dissonance,[43] others like Amy Gutmann and Dennis Thompson or Seyla Benhabib admit that individuals sometimes use self-serving arguments in public but as a general matter of political culture these are often difficult to sustain.[44]

While deliberative democrats see transparency of political decision-making as a factor contributing to the quality and public-spirited character of political decisions, empirical findings to this effect are inconclusive. Research reveals that under the public eye, decision-makers may become more concerned to please their electorate, gain favor with the voters, and score political points against their opponents rather than find the best solution to the policy issue at hand. Because they know that their positions are closely followed, they have an incentive to say what their audiences want to hear rather than to defend the policy proposals they judge best. They are less likely to take controversial positions and, for fear of losing face, less eager to make trade-offs that would make them unpopular with their electorate, even if they judge such trade-offs necessary to reach broader political goals. In front of the cameras, they engage in political messaging rather than policy-making,[45] succumb to "plebiscitary rhetoric,"[46] and resort to posturing and excessively hardline positions. This stymies the frankness and candor of political deliberation and puts compromise under strain, leading to a loss of efficiency in policy-making.[47] These findings qualify the optimism of transparency advocates demonstrating that the effect of transparency on the quality of decision-making is ambivalent: it may improve the quality of political deliberation, but it may also negatively affect it.

2.3 Interim conclusion: the mixed blessings of transparency

Measured in terms of its effects on the quality of governance, transparency is a mixed bag. "For every example . . . where transparency seemed to produce more accountable and effective governance," Stephen Kosack and Archon Fung report in their review of recent empirical research, "there is another where transparency either had no effect or produced a backlash."[48] If the positive effects of transparency are outweighed by its negative effects, insisting on transparency seems unreasonable. In those cases, one may have good consequentialist reasons to avoid fully transparent procedures.[49] Consequentialist-minded proponents of transparency, then, must be committed to making room for a degree of secrecy in democratic governance.

2.4 Non-consequentialist arguments for transparency

Empirical findings may well qualify the categorical presumption in favor of transparency if it is articulated in terms of transparency's beneficial consequences but not so when it is spelled out in terms of non-consequentialist arguments. Non-consequentialist arguments for transparency are less sensitive to its actual consequences. On the non-consequentialist view, there are considerations that the state cannot fail to realize even if realizing them will bring about more disutility than utility. These considerations instantiate certain unconditional moral principles or people's rights. Advocates of open government often take transparency to belong to this class: according to them, transparency ought to unconditionally govern the state's actions toward its members because it verifies the justice of the state's actions or because it is a matter of respecting the "people's right to know." Similarly, there are certain actions that, no matter how morally good their consequences, are morally wrong. Secrecy is a token of injustice and violates the "people's right to know" and, thus, no matter how beneficial the consequences it can bring about, it should not be adopted.

Non-consequentialist arguments in favor of transparency have received only cursory treatment in transparency scholarship. The following discussion is meant to give them the place they deserve in this discourse. I pay special attention to the argument presenting transparency as a matter of people's rights, which is regularly present in the legal rhetoric of different law systems and in court cases dealing with FOIA requests. I conclude that just like the consequentialist defense of transparency its non-consequentialist defense must also be committed to making room for secrecy in governance.

2.4.1 Transparency as a token of justice

One non-consequentialist argument presents government transparency as a matter of the justice of government actions. This defense of transparency is anchored in Kant's discussion of the principle of publicity. Kant expounds this principle in "Perpetual Peace" presenting it as a test that any policy must pass in order to be morally permissible: "All actions relating to the right of other human beings are unjust if their maxim is not consistent with publicity."[50]

Kant's principle of publicity is a test of the justice of laws and policies in much the same way in which the universal law formula of the categorical imperative is a test of the moral permissiveness of individual maxims. The universal law formula of the categorical imperative asks whether in the hypothetical situation in which the maxim became a universal law, its realization would be possible without thereby frustrating itself. It is designed to exclude those maxims, which depend on exemption from universality in order to succeed. This exemption from the universality of law is what Kant sees as constitutive of injustice. The publicity principle, similarly to the universality test, is meant to rule out, as unjust, maxims of intended political action which, if disclosed, would frustrate their aims.[51] That the maxim, if made public, would defeat its aims is an indicator of injustice: a policy the maxim of which can succeed only in secret is wrong.

At first sight, the test seems to denounce all state secrets as unjust. This appearance has prompted many to see the publicity principle as an early attempt to affirm the moral importance of transparency in political decision-making and to read Kant as a radical democratic theorist of open government.[52] However, the scope of transparency in politics Kant's principle makes imperative is limited.

First, the publicity test is designed merely as "an experiment of pure reason,"[53] a hypothetical test that can be performed regardless of the actual disclosure to an existing public. According to the principle, a maxim of intended political action is permissible if the public, upon learning the maxim, would not oppose it and frustrate its aims. Note that even if a maxim is kept secret, its actual secrecy is compatible with the possibility that *if it were disclosed* it would be accepted by the public.[54] As a consequence of making the publicity test a hypothetical rather than an empirical test that policies must meet in order to be permissible, it is thus possible that secret maxims will pass the publicity test. Hypothetical transparency, that is, does not preclude actual secrecy. As Kevin Davis observes, by presenting publicity as "a transcendental condition of justice, Kant actually permits extreme degrees of secrecy . . . in politics. . . . Though Kant requires just actions to be capable of publicity, this principle by no means sanctions action against government that legislates in secrecy."[55]

Second, as David Luban,[56] Axel Gosseries, and Tom Parr[57] observe, Kant does not give an indication regarding the level of generality at which maxims ought to be tested. However, they argue, the scope of transparency in politics required by the publicity principle depends on the level of generality at which it tests maxims of intended political action. The lower the level of generality at which maxims are formulated and tested, the higher the risk that the publicity principle becomes over-exclusive excluding, as unjust, policies that are nonetheless the right thing to do. An example is a covert police operation to catch criminals. This policy cannot succeed without secrecy: if the police revealed the details of its covert operation to catch criminals, this information would allow criminals to change their whereabouts, thereby defeating the point of the operation. While the operation can succeed only in secret and, hence, fails the publicity test, we would not judge it unjust. This and similar examples of over-exclusiveness of the publicity principle call it into question as a test of justice of political decisions because they demonstrate that a good policy becomes inconceivable in a world governed by it. In order to avoid being over-exclusive, the publicity principle should allow testing maxims at a higher level of generality at which they articulate reasons for violating the principle when publicity would defeat their purpose. In terms of the example of covert police action, a second-order maxim would read: "The police may adopt policies that violate the publicity principle if this is the only way to enforce law and catch criminals." If this second-order maxim allowing for first-order secrecy is capable of being publicly proclaimed without frustrating itself, the intended resort to first-order secrecy would be morally permissible.[58] Formulated in this way, however, the publicity principle permits a degree of secrecy in governance.

In light of the arguments above, the publicity principle does not rule out all state secrecy. The normative defense of transparency predicated on the publicity principle must likewise make room for a degree of secrecy in governance.

2.4.2 Transparency and the people's right to know

According to a second non-consequentialist defense of transparency, transparency legislation testifies to the people's "right to know."[59] The people's right to know is understood as a right held by any individual, as against his/her government, to know about its workings and dealings.[60] There is a wide agreement that rights provide reasons that are particularly weighty in that they entitle their holders to act in certain ways and give reasons to treat them in certain ways even if some social aim would be served by doing otherwise. Insofar as rights are "trumps"[61] overriding reasons of other sorts, the people's right to know government information trumps any advantages that state secrecy may bring about. As state secrecy offends against the people's right to know, it should be abandoned. Indeed, to the extent that rights correlate with duties, the people's right to know implies a duty on the part of the government to disclose information.

The people's "right to know" was among ideas that led to the adoption of FOIA legislation.[62] As envisaged by its early advocates, the people's right to know was a fairly sweeping right. According to Thomas Emerson, for example, the right to know extended "to all information in the possession of the government. . . . As a general proposition there would be no holding back of information."[63] Only the "most urgent public necessity"[64] could justify the state's resort to secrecy. Such insurgent transparency rhetoric has in recent years been appropriated by WikiLeaks. In dumping gigabytes of leaked government information online, WikiLeaks presents itself as a radical enforcer of the people's right to know. Making total elimination of state secrecy its aim, "WikiLeaks," Assange claims, "can enforce the . . . right to know, the right to speak, and, above all, the right to communicate information."[65]

Next, I examine two versions of the argument that present the right to know information within government control as, respectively, a human right and a right of citizenship. I argue that each of them must be committed to making space for secrecy in governance.

2.4.2.1 The people's right to know as a human right

In his defense of transparency in politics, Patrick Birkinshaw claims that access to government-held information is "fundamental to my membership as a full member of the human race."[66] Similar claims figure in a number of legal and political documents. Under the heading of freedom of speech, the Universal Declaration of Human Rights (UDHR) and the European Convention of Human Rights (ECHR) recognize a general human right to seek, receive, and impart information, which courts have come to interpret as a right to know. Recent jurisdiction of the European Court of Human Rights (ECtHR) makes clear that the human right to seek and receive information conceived in such broad terms involves access to government information. In 2013, the Court's judgment granted a Belgrade-based NGO a right to access classified intelligence information held by the Serbian Intelligence Agency on the grounds of Article 10 (App. No. 48135/06). Ordering the Serbian Intelligence Agency to make the requested information accessible to the applicant NGO on the grounds of the article protecting a freedom to receive information, the ECtHR effectively recognized access to intelligence information as a matter of the human right to know.

The assertion that access to government-held information is a matter of a human right raises a number of questions. Why is an interest in receiving information a matter of human rights in the first place? Do we have a human right to know simpliciter, or a right to know only certain kinds of information? If only certain kinds of information, why would government or, for that matter, intelligence information fall within that range?

In order to understand the rationale behind conceiving of transparency as a human right, we need to turn to theories of human rights.

2.4.2.1.1 THE NATURALISTIC CONCEPTION

A long-standing tradition in understanding human rights is to conceive of them on a model of natural rights. First, as with natural rights, people possess human rights simply in virtue of their humanity. Second, human rights, like natural rights, are universal. Relatedly, they exist prior to and independently of any social or political arrangements; their validity does not depend on their recognition by political society.

It is not immediately clear in what sense a claim to access government information, including intelligence information, satisfies this description. First, what human interests of paramount importance are at stake in accessing government information? Proponents of the naturalistic approach claim that all human rights are generated out of the urgent and universal interest in the exercise of human agency, such as people's capacity for autonomy.[67] This, presumably, must also hold true for the right to access information within government control. An argument to this effect could begin by emphasizing that access to information is a prerequisite for the capacity to make autonomous choices. In a second step, one could argue that information within government control belongs with the information necessary for the capacity to make autonomous choices.

Second, in what sense is the right to access government information a universal right? Given that the right to access government information is tied to existing political institutions – for example, governments and their intelligence services – how can it be binding at all times and all places? To echo Joseph Raz's challenge, "[I]t follows that cave dwellers in the Stone Age had that right. Does that make sense?"[68] Proponents of the naturalistic approach have a ready answer to this concern. They speak of human rights at different levels of abstraction. For example, James Griffin speaks of basic and derived human rights. Basic human rights refer to general moral claims made on behalf of human agency. Derived rights "come about as a result of the application of these highest-level considerations with increasing attention to circumstances."[69] In light of these arguments, the institutional embedding of the human right to know government information is not inconsistent with the universal character of human rights. Rather, its institutional form is the form that the universal basic human right to information acquires in circumstances in which government institutions shape the conditions in which people live. As no such institutions shaped the circumstances in which Stone Age cave dwellers used to live, it would indeed be absurd to claim that they had a human right to access government information. We can nonetheless argue that even Stone Age cave dwellers had a generic version of this right – namely, a human right to information relevant to their circumstances.

On the naturalistic approach, then, the argument that access to government-held information in liberal-democratic societies is a human right would take the following form: (1) access to information necessary for autonomous action is a human right and (2) under the conditions of modern societies, government information is information of this necessary kind. Hence (3) access to government information is a human right.

Whether the conclusion (3) holds depends on whether the move from step (1) to step (2) is warranted; that is, it depends on how one goes about specifying the general moral claim to information necessary for autonomous action in modern societies. Under the conditions of pluralism and disagreement that characterize modern societies, general moral claims can be specified in many different and competing ways. Starting with disagreements about the value of autonomy and conditions for autonomous action, people will disagree about what information they need in order to act in an autonomous way. Some may consider intelligence information necessary to make autonomous political choices; others may not. Those who agree that intelligence information is necessary to make autonomous political choices will disagree about the scope of that information. If information about electronic surveillance is necessary to make autonomous political choices, is all other intelligence information similarly necessary? If only some of it is, which? What other information within government control is similarly necessary? Diplomatic cables? Internal memos?

The few human rights theorists who have addressed this problem deal with it by reference to political decision-making. According to Seyla Benhabib, in the face of disagreement regarding the content of human rights, we should resort to the process of democratic decision-making to resolve it.[70] As Samantha Besson says, it is "the law [that] turns universal moral rights into human rights."[71] If political decision-making and national legislation specify the content of human rights, then, national FOIA legislation emerges as the specification mechanism translating a general moral right to information relevant to one's circumstances into action-guiding principles under typical social-political conditions of modern societies. Remarkably, a closer analysis of the ECtHR judgment in the Serbian case adds plausibility to this argument. The applicant NGO lodged the case at the ECtHR after the Serbian Intelligence Agency did not comply with the decision of the Serbian Information Commissioner in its favor. In its judgment, the Court invoked the fact that the Serbian Information Commissioner had ordered disclosure of the classified documents. It was the "obstinate reluctance" of the Serbian Intelligence Agency to comply with this declassification order that, in the Court's judgment, constituted a breach of Article 10 of the Convention (App. No. 48135/06, para. 26). Now, if the Court perceived a violation of a domestic FOIA legislation as equivalent to a violation of a human right to know, then the Court took domestic information law to specify the human right to know.

This answer to the specification problem has important consequences for the scope of the human right to access government-held information. If resolving a disagreement about the boundaries of the human right to know is a matter of a political decision, then, ultimately, it is the political decision-maker – a political actor with law-making and law-amendment powers – that determines the exact contents of the human right to know. Even if the human right to know has a normative status prior to political decision-making, it is the outcome of political decision-making that determines which information, including government information, people are entitled to know in virtue of this right. This is to concede that the political decision-maker may exempt certain information, including government information, from its scope. In exempting certain government information from the scope of information that people are entitled to access, the political decision-maker establishes a class of information to which government is not obliged to grant access. The process in which the people's right to know acquires its content, then, is the same process that sets limits to this right, that is, establishes a domain of state secrecy. This co-originality of transparency and secrecy in politics explains what Tero Erkkilä flags as a paradoxical feature of freedom of information legislation: "One paradoxical characteristic of information access laws is that oftentimes they are actually secrecy laws, defining the limits of the public through exemption, that is, what is not public."[72] I conclude that the argument defending transparency in terms of a human right to know must be committed to acknowledging the co-originality of transparency and secrecy in governance. To acknowledge the co-originality of transparency and secrecy in governance is to acknowledge that the same moral principles that ground the people's right to access government information also establish a domain of state secrecy. This must commit proponents of this defense of transparency to making room for secrecy in governance.

2.4.2.1.2 THE POLITICAL CONCEPTION

A second influential account of human rights, introduced by John Rawls, is "political, not metaphysical" in that it is worked out independently of any substantial foundation in "a theological, philosophical, or moral conception of the nature of the human person."[73] This account of human rights takes as its core idea the practical role that human rights are to play in the international order.

According to the political conception, human rights introduce a system of standards for the domestic conduct of governments with regard to their citizens that reasonable states would agree to adopt even if they disagreed about their justification. They would incorporate them as a "module" in their legal regimes from within their different political moralities and ethical outlooks. As Rawls puts it, the satisfaction of such norms is a condition of a state having its "internal sovereignty"[74] respected; their violation justifies international intervention. Joshua Cohen links human rights so understood to principles of legitimate political authority.[75] The idea is that states would incorporate such pre-institutional moral norms regulating their relationships with their citizens lest they lose their claim to legitimacy.

From this perspective, to claim that access to government information is a human right is to claim that access to government information is a pre-institutional moral right to which every reasonable state would give effect in its national legislation lest it lose its claim to legitimacy. Just as in the naturalistic conception, then, a human right to access government information acquires its specific content and scope in national legislation. To repeat the conclusion reached in the previous section, the people's right to know and state secrecy, emerging from the same process of institutionalizing the human right to know, are co-original. To the extent that proponents of the human-rights-defense of transparency must be committed to acknowledging the co-originality of transparency and secrecy in governance, they must also be committed to making room for secrecy in governance.

2.4.2.2 The people's right to know as a right of citizenship

Another understanding of the people's right to know conceives of it as a right of citizenship. In his defense of transparency in governance, Birkinshaw appeals to it in one breath with an appeal to human rights: "The right to information . . . is fundamental to my position as a citizen and a human being."[76] Similarly, the 2004 Joint Declaration by the United Nations Special Rapporteur on Freedom of Opinion and Expression, the OSCE Representative on Freedom of the Media, and the OAS Special Rapporteur on Freedom of Expression appeal in its first paragraph to human rights as the grounds of the right to access information held by public authorities and in its third paragraph states that "[a]ccess to information is a citizens' right."[77] A similar proclamation is made by the EU Charter of Fundamental Rights.

To claim that access to government-held information is a right of citizenship is to claim that it is a special right that arises on the plane of relations between citizens and the state. A model that has been widely used to illuminate the relation between citizens and the state in a representative democracy is the model of the principal-agent relation. In this relation, one party (citizens-principals) empowers another (state actors-agents) to represent her interests and to act on her behalf, and the latter provides an account of her actions with respect to those interests.[78] This relation of political representation is commonly analyzed along two dimensions. First, state actors-agents exercise authority over citizens when acting on their behalf and in light of their interests. Second, citizens-principals call state actors to account. Next, I argue that citizenship conceived along these two dimensions grounds the people's right to know but also limits it by establishing a domain of state secrecy.

The way the accountability requirement bears on the people's right to know is straightforward. Calling the state-agent to account is meant to establish whether it exercises authority in accordance with the mandate conferred upon it by the citizens-principals. On one line of argument, people have a right to access government-held information whenever they suspect that office holders abuse their mandate: their right to access government information is a check on abuse of power. On the second line of argument, people need not suspect misconduct in order to justify their right to access government information; rather, they have a right to know the conduct of government business because, as Jeremy Waldron put it, "[I]t is their business conducted in their name."[79] Some scholars would go so far as to say that the information within government control is the citizens' property. As owners of government information, they are entitled to access it at any time. For instance, Roy Peled and Yoram Rabin claim:

> Information held by public authorities is, in fact, the property of state's citizens. . . . The information held by public agencies was 'created' or gathered by civil servants-officials . . . who carry out their mandate by means of taxes paid to the public. By the very nature of this structure, the owners of the information, those who financed its collection, should have access to it.[80]

Whereas the link between accountability and the people's right to know has been widely discussed, only a few scholars have paid attention to the link between the people's right to know and the second dimension of citizenship – namely, the people's subjection to political authority. Bernard Manin, Adam Przeworski, and Susan Stokes point out that to the extent that state actors have the authority to rule, they also have the authority to establish rules of information access:

> The peculiarity of the principal-agent relation entailed in the relation of political representation is that our agents are our rulers: we designate them as agents so that they would tell us what to do, and we even give them the authority to coerce us to do it. And the rules that our agents impose on us include access to information. . . . The principal-agent model entailed in the relation of representation is a peculiar one, insofar as it is the agents who decide what principals will know about their actions.[81]

If state actors have the authority to establish rules of information access, they have the authority to classify information, that is, to limit the scope of the right to know that people have in their capacity as citizens-principals and the scope of government transparency corresponding to that right. Accordingly, citizens have no right to know information that they, in their capacity as principals, have authorized their representatives-agents to classify.

The two dimensions of citizenship that shape the people's right to know seem to pull in opposite directions and, insofar as the limits on the people's right to know (authority-dimension) prevent citizens from accessing information required to call office holders to account (accountability-dimension), they seem to build in a contradiction at its heart. Whether the contradiction is real depends on whether limits to transparency indeed inhibit accountability. The discussion about the nexus between transparency and accountability is extensive, and I will address it in more detail in Chapters 5 and 6. At this point suffice it to say that whereas transparency may be an instrument of accountability, it is not its necessary condition. As Rahul Sagar argues, to ensure accountability for secret decisions and processes "democracies must provide citizens either with access to withheld information or the confidence that it has been withheld for legitimate purposes."[82] Controlling whether information has been withheld for legitimate reasons does not require disclosing it to public view. Rather than to the people at large, it can be disclosed to discrete groups of people, for example, specialized parliamentary or judicial committees acting on behalf of citizens. Provided that oversight mechanisms are successful, the tension between the two dimensions of citizenship need not render the people's right to know government information inconsistent. Rather, it implies that the same principle of citizenship that establishes it also determines its limits. In limiting it, it also establishes a domain of state secrecy. The co-originality of transparency and secrecy, as anchored in the principle of citizenship, must commit proponents of this argument to make room for secrecy in governance.

2.5 Conclusion

In this chapter, I have reflected on the normative grounds and limits of the political imperative of transparency. Having considered consequentialist arguments underpinning the demands for greater transparency in democratic governance, I have found them less categorical than their proponents take them to be. Next to positive effects, transparency may also have adverse effects on governance. To the extent that transparency may generate disutility, consequentialist-minded proponents of transparency must be committed to making room for secrecy in governance.

Non-consequentialist arguments for transparency likewise imply space for secrecy in governance. Presenting transparency as a token of justice and a matter of human and civil rights, they establish the political imperative of transparency, but they also establish exemptions and limits to it. In that, they establish a domain of state secrecy.

If both the consequentialist and non-consequentialist arguments for transparency are committed to concede a degree of secrecy in politics, does this mean that a degree of secrecy in governance can be legitimate? The next chapters explore this question.

Notes

1 Rosanvallon 2008, 258.
2 The White House 2009, 1.

3 https://eur-lex.europa.eu/legal-content/EN/TXT/?uri=LEGISSUM%3Aai0003
4 www.oecd.org/unitedstates/opennessandtransparency-pillarsfordemocracytrustandprogress.htm
5 Naurin 2006, 91; Meijer 2013, 430.
6 Fenster 2015, 151.
7 Davis 1998, 121. Journalists and advocates of open government are among the strongest adherents of transparency; see Fenster 2017, 207.
8 But see Naurin 2006 for conceptual distinctions between publicity and transparency.
9 Bentham 1843, 145.
10 For a discussion of Bentham's defense of transparency, see Baume and Papadopoulos 2018.
11 De Fine Licht 2020. See also Alloa 2018, 32.
12 Roberts 2006(b), 110–112; Murray 2005, 201; Novak 2023.
13 Thomas 2020, 87.
14 https://nos.nl/nieuwsuur/artikel/2437332-ministeries-betaalden-volkskrant-bijna-ton-voor-te-laat-delen-informatie
15 Hafner-Burton 2008.
16 Bauhr and Grimes 2014, 300.
17 Bauhr and Grimes 2014.
18 The White House 2009, 1.
19 Brin 1998; Hood and Heald 2006.
20 Levi, Sacks and Tyler 2009; De Fine Licht 2013.
21 Bentham 1843, 30.
22 Mendelberg 2002; Thompson 2008.
23 Wang and Guan 2022, 1.
24 Worthy 2010, 572.
25 O'Neill 2002, 72–73; Meijer, 't Hart and Worthy 2018, 504.
26 Domscheit-Berg 2011, 174–175; Roberts 2012, 122.
27 Cucciniello, Porumbescu and Grimmelikhuijsen 2017.
28 De Fine Licht 2020, 21–23.
29 Bovens 2003; Fung and Weil 2010, 106.
30 Worthy 2010, 576.
31 Roberts 2006(b), 119.
32 Meijer, 't Hart and Worthy 2018, 510.
33 Wang and Guan 2022, 13.
34 The White House 2009, 1.
35 Naurin 2006.
36 Worthy 2020, 46.
37 Mill 1962.
38 Mill 1962, 214.
39 Cohen 1997; Gutmann and Thompson 2004.
40 Bok 1984, 114.
41 Benhabib 1996, 72; Cohen 1997, 76–77.
42 Chambers 2004, 391. Emphasis added.
43 Dryzek 2000, 46–47; Elster 1997, 12.
44 Gutmann and Thompson 1996, 126–127; Benhabib 1996.
45 Lee 2019.
46 Chambers 2004, 389.
47 Elster 1997; Chambers 2004; Lee 2019.
48 Kosack and Fung 2014, 66.
49 De Fine Licht 2020, 25.
50 Kant 1957/1795, 129.
51 Kant 1983, 135–136.

52 Williams 1983; Clinger 2017.
53 Kant 1957/1795.
54 The concept of "the public" invoked by Kant's publicity principle is ambiguous. As Davis (1991, 418) explains, the publicity test as a test of the moral acceptability of policy could not refer to an actual public because there is no guarantee that an actual public is a good judge of the morality of the policies: any actual public may demand purely unjust policies. Thus, the nature of the publicity test seems to require an ideal public of rational agents. However, when discussing examples of the publicity test at work, Kant refers to a non-ideal public. Whereas the exact character of "the public" will not affect the possibility of secret maxims passing the publicity test, it will affect which secret maxims may do so.
55 Davis 1991, 410, 417.
56 Luban 1996.
57 Gosseries and Parr 2021.
58 Luban 1996, 188–191.
59 This section draws from Mokrosinska 2018.
60 Cf. Schauer 1983, 70; Henkin 1971 discusses this argument in the context of the Pentagon Papers.
61 Dworkin 1984.
62 Fenster 2017.
63 Emerson 1976, 14–16.
64 Cross 1953, xiv.
65 Assange cited in Fenster 2021, 65.
66 Birkinshaw 2006, 56.
67 Griffin 2008.
68 Raz 2010, 40.
69 Griffin 2008, 50.
70 Benhabib 2011, 65.
71 Besson 2014, 284.
72 Erkkilä 2020, 8.
73 Rawls 1999, 81.
74 Rawls 1999, 79.
75 Cohen 2006, 234.
76 Birkinshaw 2006, 56.
77 Ligabo, Duve and Bertoni 2003.
78 Pitkin 1967; Christiano 1996.
79 Waldron 2016, 183.
80 Peled and Rabin 2011, 365.
81 Przeworski, Manin and Stokes 1999, 24.
82 Sagar 2007, 421.

3 Reclaiming raison d'état

The necessity of executive secrecy[1]

3.1 Introduction

If the political imperative of transparency is less categorical than assumed, does this mean that secrecy in democratic governance can be legitimate? Focusing on executive secrecy, this chapter explores an argument according to which secrecy is a necessary measure called for in exceptional circumstances in which the basic interests of the state are at stake.

The appeal to necessity is a recurrent rationale for government secrecy to which executive branch officials regularly resort in political practice. For example, when the UK government refused to disclose the British Cabinet minutes from March 2003, in which military action in Iraq was deliberated, it claimed that withholding information was necessary to ensure the effective operation of Cabinet government. In the Statement of Reasons declining the request for disclosure submitted by the Iraq Inquiry Committee and an FOI campaigner, the Attorney General argued that:

> Conventions on Cabinet confidentiality are of the greatest pertinence when the issues at hand are of the greatest sensitivity. . . . Disclosure of Cabinet minutes . . . has the potential to . . . compromise the integrity of this thinking space where it is most needed.[2]

Besides arguments presenting secrecy as a necessary tool ensuring the government's capacity for decision and action, there are arguments that present secrecy as a necessary condition of national security. For example, when the Polish government refused to either confirm or deny the existence of the CIA black sites on its territory between 2002 and 2004, it claimed that secrecy about its collaboration in the secret CIA extraordinary rendition program was necessary for national security. While Poland's participation in the program was not motivated by terrorism threats to its national security, Polish decision-makers at the time saw alliance with the United States as a strategic national security guarantee against Russia.[3] Since "the interest of the Polish state [was] based on necessity to participate in the anti-terrorist coalition" according to

DOI: 10.4324/9781003083733-3

the Polish Prime Minister,[4] and since the US – PL intelligence cooperation fell under NATO's Cosmic Top Secret classification, secrecy was deemed necessary to national security.

"Political survival" in the face of national security threats and "government capacity for action" are two dominant narratives in terms of which the necessity argument has been framed. Each of them, as proponents of the necessity argument claim, makes a convincing case that government's resort to secrecy is a legitimate exercise of democratic authority. The purpose of this chapter is to normatively assess this claim. When secrecy is necessary for democratic states to survive and effectively operate, is it thereby democratically legitimate? Does necessity render secrecy legitimate?

The argument unfolds as follows. I start, in Sections 3.2 and 3.3, by homing in on the two forms of the necessity argument. In Section 3.4, I argue that in both versions, the argument follows the logic of the raison d'état tradition. That tradition is antithetical to democracy in that it conceives of secrecy, along with other special powers adopted by the state in situations of necessity, as creating a space for an exercise of power devoid of the moral and legal principles that govern liberal-democratic states. Section 3.5 explores a claim made by proponents of the necessity argument that the suspension of moral and legal principles in situations of necessity is not antithetical to democracy when it serves certain democratic values. This claim, if plausible, could enable the necessity argument to escape the anti-democratic implications that pertain to the reason of state tradition. In Section 3.6, I examine this democratized version of reason of state argument from the perspective of political morality. In Section 3.7, I consider it from the perspective of legal theory. I argue that an appeal to necessity cannot be codified in terms of the moral and legal principles that the political authority exercised by democratic governments presupposes. This leads me to conclude in Section 3.8 that the necessity argument fails to present secrecy as an exercise of democratic authority and fails to escape the anti-democratic implications of reason of state thinking. Necessary secrets, contrary to what proponents of the necessity argument claim, are not a legitimate form of democratic governance. With regard to my opening examples, this implies that neither the UK government's withholding of Cabinet minutes regarding the Iraq war nor the Polish government's refusal to confirm or deny its involvement with the CIA can enjoy democratic legitimacy in virtue of them being necessary for, respectively, the government's capacity for effective decision-making and national security. I do not mean to deny that executive secrecy in situations of necessity can ever be legitimate but only that an appeal to necessity will not legitimate it.

3.2 Secrecy and the political survival of the state

In its first narrative, the necessity argument presents secrecy as an emergency measure employed in order to ensure the political survival of the state. The emergency rationale is tightly linked to national security. It draws on the idea, deeply embedded in bureaucratic and popular culture, that the defense of national security demands strict controls on the flow of information.[5] In situations of national security crises, such as terrorist threat, invasion, or war, disclosure of certain classes of information would make the state vulnerable, for example, making troop positions public would make them an easy target for the enemy. In her recent work, Cécile Fabre defends secrecy in the context of military and economic espionage and intelligence along these lines.[6] The appropriation and disclosure of sources and methods of intelligence would expose them to countermeasures, thus threatening individual and collective security and "members' collective political agency";[7] in such situations, Fabre argues, resorting to secrecy is justified, provided it is proportional to the threat it is meant to avert and is effective in doing so.

Diplomatic relations are another policy area of which secrecy is considered an integral part. Diplomatic documents, when misused, can harm the vital interests of the state. Thus, even though democratic states commonly recognize a right to access to information, they also widely accept a diplomatic exception to it (e.g., the doctrine of executive privilege (US), the public interest immunity (UK), or the principle of *diplomatie secrète* (France)). In general, as Mai'a Cross argues, secrecy is accepted "in the crafting of national foreign policy because it pertains to survival of the state, which is core to national sovereignty."[8]

The emergency framing of the necessity argument has traditionally focused on policy areas dealing with national security and defense. Over the past decades, however, security and defense factors have been presented as interrelated with other political, economic, and social factors allowing the presentation of issues that go beyond questions of traditional security as potential security threats.[9] As a result of such "securitization" of public policies, the necessity argument has expanded to policy domains ranging from migration, energy, climate change, and critical infrastructure, to public health and finance.[10] For example, scholars point out that the British Security Service Act of 1989 imposes on the security service the function of "safeguard[ing] the economic well-being" of the nation; the US National Security Education Act of 1991 similarly makes a direct connection between national security and the "economic well-being of the United States."[11] As the scope of national security issues expands so does the scope of emergency powers, including secrecy. For example, calling immigration a "threat to national security" in European programs of border surveillance and migration policy has opened the door to state secrecy in migration policy enforcement.[12]

3.3 Secrecy and the executive capacity for action

While the first necessity rationale of executive secrecy presents secrecy as a condition of the political survival of the state, the second presents secrecy as a necessary condition of the effectiveness of government action. "[S]ome democratic policies require secrecy," Dennis Thompson writes, "if they were made public, [they] could not be carried out as effectively or at all."[13] The two frames overlap. For example, in the realm of security and defense, secrecy is a strategic resource employed to enhance the effectiveness of intelligence sources and methods. Given the role of intelligence sources and methods in national security, its effectiveness therein is also a matter of political survival.

In policy areas other than defense and security, the effectiveness rationale of state secrecy often stands on its own. In economic policy, secrecy is presented as a condition of the effectiveness of government financial market interventions such as currency devaluation or price decontrol.[14] It is also invoked as a condition of the effectiveness of government action in the realm of law enforcement: the police could not infiltrate criminal networks if it revealed in advance where it is going to place undercover agents and how to recognize them.[15]

The effectiveness rationale is also invoked to justify the secrecy of the deliberations of executive bodies. A number of policy-oriented studies demonstrate that opening decision-making processes to the wider public and the media, by exposing decision-makers to external pressures, lowers the quality of policy discussions and increases the likelihood of negotiation deadlock.[16] Within this view, secret settings serve the decision-making process because they insulate decision-makers from external pressures that may disrupt it. In the United States, deliberative process privilege protects from disclosure of privileged communications within or between government agencies. The need for deliberative secrecy motivates one of the exemptions to the US FOIA Act, which entitles the executive to withhold internal deliberation, policy-making, and inter- or intra-departmental records that are pre-decisional from the public view. In Germany, a similar principle is written into the constitution. The *Kernbereich exekutiver Eigenverantwortung* was introduced by the German Federal Constitutional Court in 1984 (BVerfGE 67, 101). This principle establishes a constitutional right to deliberative secrecy on the part of the executive by recognizing that the government needs a protected sphere for deliberation, free from parliamentary interference, before taking a decision.

In all these cases, the effectiveness rationale for secrecy in governance focuses on the state's capacity for action (which need not relate to averting an acute danger to national security). Given that openness would undercut it, secrecy, as a necessary condition of its success, is privileged over transparency.

3.4 Democratic deficits of secrecy

The two versions of the necessity argument present secrecy as a tool for advancing basic state interests in situations in which transparency would endanger their realization. The necessity argument encounters, however, important challenges, which relate to democratic deficits that the executive resort to secrecy brings about.

One concern about government secrecy bears on the legitimacy of decision-making processes. It is commonplace to think that in a democracy, political decisions are legitimate only if they are authorized by citizens. Denied knowledge of the state's actions, citizens cannot consent to or dissent from the state's actions. From this perspective, secret uses of power seem to lack democratic authorization because people cannot authorize what they are denied knowledge about.

A related concern is that secret policies and closed-door decision-making processes generate a knowledge deficit that undermines mechanisms of democratic accountability: people cannot control state officials and hold them to account if they do not know what these officials are doing and why. As Richard Aldrich and Daniela Richterova observe, "[S]ecrecy is often interpreted . . . as providing a discretionary space of action . . . opaque to the cleansing effect of democratic scrutiny."[17]

Executive secrecy also cuts democratic deliberation short in situations in which democratic self-governance requires it most *viz.* when reasonable people disagree about whether the situation qualifies as a necessity and about the scope of secrecy that may be required in response. This problem emerged with particular force in the context of the National Security Agency (NSA) secret surveillance program leaked by Edward Snowden. The program relied on a number of assumptions about which reasonable citizens disagree such as the level of risk to public security and the scope of the trade-offs between security and individual privacy a society is willing to accept. The secrecy of the program prevented public debate on these issues. Without it, according to Eric Boot, the NSA's unilateral decision that its intelligence function was so important to public security that it condoned violating individuals' privacy online lacked democratic legitimacy.[18]

The common denominator of the concerns flagged in the previous paragraphs is a worry about the impact of government secrecy on democratic equality and popular sovereignty. Equality of decision-making power between citizens and representatives and the idea that citizens should remain co-authors of laws and policies to which they are subject are among key democratic ideas.[19] Government secrecy leaves people out of the collective decision-making process. Excluding people from participation in the decision-making process, its authorization, and its control seems to disable the arrangements ensuring representative responsiveness to citizens' wishes. Deprived of the possibility to participate in, authorize, and control political decisions and processes, popular sovereignty and people's equal status seem threatened.

3.5 Democratized reason of state?

Whereas the state's resort to secrecy in situations of necessity violates moral and legal principles that otherwise constrain political action, proponents of the necessity argument claim that the benefits of secrecy, measured in terms of public security and/or government's capacity for action, justify this violation. Such consequentialist arguments granting the state, in situations of necessity, special powers to do something it could not otherwise do have a long history. Scholars link them to the reason of state tradition. "[T]he idea of 'reason of state'," as Nancy Rosenblum put it, "captures this tension between legal concerns and grim necessity."[20]

Reason of state doctrine emerged in early modernity and is commonly associated with Machiavelli and the thinking about politics that he instigated.[21] Secrecy has been a defining element of the reason of state doctrine since its inception.[22] A distinctive feature of reason of state politics is the recognition that serving vital interests of the state may require a violation of moral or legal norms. These norms would prevail had they not clashed with reason of state: their violation has to be tolerated as a concession to practical necessity. Friedrich Meinecke, in his classic survey of the intellectual history of the concept, put it thus:

> *Raison d'etat* is the fundamental principle of national conduct, the State's first Law of Motion. It tells the statesman what he must do to preserve the health and strength of the State. . . . The well-being of the State and of its population is held to be the ultimate value and the goal . . . which must – without any qualification – be procured. Without qualification, insofar as it must even be procured if necessary at the expense of a complete disregard for moral and positive law.[23]

The contemporary necessity defense of state secrecy reiterates this claim and in this it restates the classic doctrine of reason of state. Yet there is a caveat. Reason of state thinking has been deemed antithetical to democratic governance because the powers it confers upon the state to respond to situations of necessity are actually unlimited, standing beyond the legal order of a liberal-democratic state and devoid of democratic control. Carl Schmitt, for example, openly acknowledged the anti-democratic character of emergency powers.[24] Were the necessity argument a mere re-statement of reason of state, its proponents could not be expected to offer an account of the democratic legitimacy of the special powers of the state, which they set out to do. If anything then, they have to deny the anti-democratic character of the special powers that the state exercises in situations of necessity. Their strategy is to present "political survival" and the "effectiveness of government action" as democratic goods along with values of accountability, transparency, equality, and self-governance. As long as the ends pursued by the state are democratic, the means – the powers conferred upon the state necessary to achieve them – will be democratic too. Thus, even if the pursuit of "political survival" and the "effectiveness of government action" involves infringing on democratic accountability, equality, the people's right to self-governance and political participation, this infringement is democratically justified. Fabre's defense of secrecy in the context of national security and intelligence proceeds along these lines. She defends a "democratic right to secrecy":

> By democratic rights, I mean rights the protection of which is a necessary condition for a political community to count as a democracy. . . . Now, information the unauthorized appropriation or disclosure of which would stymie citizens' exercise of their democratic agency can legitimately be protected by a right to secrecy. . . . It is precisely because the latter protects the exercise of democratic agency that it is aptly construed as a democratic right.[25]

In this "democratized" version of the reason of state argument, the state's resort to special powers overriding the moral and legal principles underpinning the liberal-democratic order in situations of necessity is a legitimate exercise of democratic authority. This is, for example, the thrust of Gabriel Schoenfeld's defense of the Manhattan Project, a military research program that produced the first nuclear weapons undertaken during World War II in the United States. Not only was the American public kept in the dark but even those who worked on the project were often unaware of the nature of the product they were constructing. Schoenfeld claims that "self-preservation" is "the most fundamental business of democratic governance."[26] Given that the project was considered necessary for the survival of American democracy, its secret character, he argues, was legitimate; the democratic deficit pertaining to executive secrecy was offset by the positive consequences it allowed to attain.[27]

A similar argument is proposed in defense of secrecy as a means of ensuring the effectiveness of government action. Thus, one claims that the government's capacity for action is a democratic good and that the benefits of securing it outweigh the costs of sacrificing the democratic commitment to open government. Given that the costs of upholding the government's transparency, measured by the negative consequences it would bring about for the government's capacity for action, are too great for the liberal-democratic state rationally to bear, one concludes that secrecy is democratically legitimate. Along these lines, Berthold Rittberger and Klaus Goetz claim: "'Getting things done' is also a core democratic value, which – under certain circumstances – might call for privileging secrecy over transparency."[28]

This democratized version of the reason of state argument relies on balancing political survival and/or the effectiveness of government action, on the one hand, and political equality, a right to self-governance, accountability, and political participation, on the other hand. To judge the success of the necessity argument is to inquire whether the way it proposes to balance these different interests of democratic government is plausible. I argue that this argumentative strategy is problematic at the level of both philosophical and legal discourses. It fails, as a democratic defense of state secrecy, for the same reason that raison d'état politics is considered antithetical to democracy.

3.6 Necessity escapes moral codification

At the level of moral theory, the necessity argument runs up against the problem that the cost-benefit analysis at its core balances traditionally consequentialist considerations (public security and political efficiency) with deontological considerations (democratic values of equality and self-governance, the right to hold decision-makers to account). This balancing exercise is problematic because deontological considerations provide us with a reason to observe them irrespective of what beneficial consequences may follow from violating them; they resist cost-benefit analysis and the utilitarian metric that goes with it. By extending cost-benefit analysis to deontological considerations, the necessity argument effectively forces a conversion of a deontological framework into a consequentialist one. The question whether this can be done places the problem of the legitimacy of executive secrecy in the context of old disputes in moral theory.

For orthodox consequentialists, the right act in any given situation is the one that will produce the best consequences, as judged from an impersonal standpoint, which gives equal weight to the interests of everyone.[29] As consequences are the only moral currency in terms of which moral judgments are to be made, whenever the importance of political survival or effectiveness of government action outweighs the importance of accountability, the state's resort to secrecy is legitimate.[30] Orthodox deontologists believe that there are moral principles that are unconditional and may never be violated. Such principles express moral values that are incommensurable and non-exchangeable; trading them off against other values is not even conceivable as there is no common currency to make the weighing exercise possible.[31] For an orthodox deontologist, then, the necessity of political survival and/or effectiveness of state action can never legitimate the state's resort to special measures that override the deontological considerations *viz.* equality, people's right to self-governance, the right to hold office holders to account, and political participation.

Both positions suffer from a similar weakness: neither takes seriously the dilemma that may arise between, on the one hand, security and/or effectiveness of government action that require secrecy and, on the other hand, democratic equality, popular sovereignty, and citizens' right to call government to account that requires transparency. Instead, they define the dilemma out of existence.[32] An intermediate position, endorsed by most contemporary deontologists, is threshold deontology according to which deontological constraints apply so long as the negative consequences remain under a certain threshold.[33] Once the threshold is reached, consequentialist considerations dominate. For instance, once the public security threat reaches a certain intensity, accountability of office holders gives in. Fabre's defense of state secrecy is a good example of a threshold deontology position. In her argument, the threshold is expressed in terms of a proportionality requirement: once the good consequences of violating otherwise fundamental moral values are in proportion to the wrong they are meant to set right, the violation becomes permissible.[34]

The trouble with this position is that it fails to explain how deontological considerations such as the values of equality and self-governance change their unconditional character once the threshold has been reached: as Allon Harel and Assaf Sharon ask, "[I]f, as deontology assumes, consequences do not determine rightness and wrongness of actions, why does this change when their weight increases?"[35] This problem bears on our discussion concerning the state's authority to resort to special measures in the following way. Special powers claimed by the state in situations of practical necessity may require violating otherwise unconditional moral principles underpinning the political order. To claim the authority to violate such principles is to claim that there are moral principles that make their violation permissible conditional on necessity. If threshold deontology is successful in stipulating such principles, the state's resort to special measures, including secrecy, could be seen as legitimate. If threshold deontology is not successful, the state's resort to such measures has no plausible ground.

I submit that threshold deontology is incoherent. My argument draws on Harel and Sharon, who demonstrate the implausibility of threshold deontology by focusing on the threshold-level permissibility of the state's resort to torture in situations of necessity.[36] I extend their argument to the state's resort to secrecy showing that it applies to a broader scope of special measures the state adopts when confronted with situations of necessity. My contribution to this debate is to connect it to the discourse on the authoritative powers of the state: I argue that in the absence of moral principles supporting threshold deontology, the state's resort to special measures (secrecy, torture, etc.) cannot be seen as an exercise of political authority.

Threshold deontology carves out space for violations in the otherwise unconditional principles once the threshold of necessity is reached. Violation presents itself as a legitimate option. Two problems emerge. First, once we grant that it is permissible to violate moral principles when the necessity threshold has been reached, the status of the threshold is eroded. Imagine that a new threat arises which the threshold model did not foresee. In this case, it is not clear whether a departure from the principle is permissible. To justify action in these circumstances, the content of the threshold rule should be specified. Under the conditions of pluralism and disagreement that characterize modern societies, this can be done in different and competing ways, which presents us with the necessity of settling on one. In Chapter 2, we encountered this problem with regard to the underdetermined content of human rights *viz.* the human right to know. The solution, as forcefully argued by many scholars, especially Kantians, is political: the state is an impartial arbiter charged with laying down the content of the right action and addressing any residual indeterminacy in cases of conflict.[37] If specifying the threshold of a permissible violation of moral principles is a matter of political decision-making, what if decision-makers conclude that adequately addressing the new threat requires lowering the threshold of permissibility for violating moral principles? Since any subsequent threat may be argued to require overriding the previous threshold, this sends the argument down the slippery slope of hollowing out moral principles until they are effectively overridden. Making the permissibility of violations of moral principles conditional on necessity makes it hard to constrain them. The same problem pertains to arguments appealing to the proportionality principle, as in Fabre's defense of secrecy. The importance of addressing the new threat may be judged so pressing as to make the relative value of countervailing considerations fade whereby the existing proportionality calculations erode. Being a different way of expressing the threshold condition, the proportionality principle also involves the possibility of its own suspension.

In political practice, such concerns resonate with the concerns voiced by activists and scholars about the unlimited powers that special measures confer on the state. Regarding executive secrecy, they indicate that the ease with which government officials "exaggerat[e] the need for secrecy"[38] sends government classification practices down a slippery slope toward overclassification *viz.* withholding information in an ever-expanding range of situations in which the necessity of secrecy is increasingly problematic. As Mark Fenster observed, the WikiLeaks and Snowden megaleaks offered an opportunity to test the government's appeals to the necessity of secrecy. The outcome, he claims, does not support government's claims made about the necessity of keeping the relevant information secret.[39]

A similar concern was raised in response to the UK government's refusal to release the official minutes of Cabinet meetings regarding British involvement in the Iraq war, as per the example opening this chapter. Arguing that disclosure would have a negative impact on the quality of future Cabinet deliberations, the government resorted to a veto power contained in section 53 of the FOIA that allows the executive to block disclosure in "exceptional circumstances".[40] Commenting on the refusal, the Information Commissioner (the UK's independent regulatory authority for information rights) observed that the veto contained a danger of sending government secrecy on a slippery slope toward permanent withholding of minutes of Cabinet discussions:

> If the veto continues to be exercised in response to the majority of orders for the disclosure of Cabinet minutes, it is hard to imagine how the most significant proceedings of the Cabinet will *ever* be made known before the elapse of 30 years . . . it seems that [such] disclosures . . . will, by definition, always be the ones to attract the veto as an 'exceptional case'.[41]

The second problem that emerges once threshold deontology builds a deviation space into the otherwise unconditional principles is that we treat unconditional principles as if they were conditional. In this, we mold them into a consequentialist framework and deny their deontological status or, as Jeremy Waldron put it, we stretch and deform them.[42] This corrupts the practical reasoning of the agents and changes our moral and political landscape beyond recognition. Harel and Sharon ask us to imagine a situation in which resorting to torture would avert a catastrophe.[43] By incorporating a principled exception to the rule prohibiting torture, an agent who considers what to do in a particular case is invited to consider the possibility that torture is permissible. Even when torture is eventually rejected on the grounds that the circumstances do not call for it, its permissibility has been elevated to the status of a rule-like directive. They argue that this would corrupt an agent's practical reasoning because the agent considers a rule permitting torture and a rule prohibiting it to be on a par whereas, when the circumstances do not justify torture, torture ought not to be merely rejected, but it need not even be considered as an option that is to be weighed against other alternatives.

If violations of unconditional moral principles were incorporated into the moral system as principled permissions under a moral rule, they would create rights to act accordingly. In the case of torture conditional on the necessity to avoid a catastrophe, this would create a right to torture others. Once we make it legitimate for the state to exercise this right on the grounds of public security, we make it legitimate for it to treat the people's right to bodily integrity and their human right not to be tortured as conditional. Such a state would not be the liberal-democratic state we are familiar with.

The thrust of all this is that no moral principle can make it morally permissible to do what is otherwise impermissible. In other words, necessity requirements escape codification in terms of moral principles or, as Aquinas put it, "necessity knows no law" (*necessitas non habet legem*).[44] If no moral principle suspending moral principles is possible, no such principle could underpin the authority of the state to resort to special measures that violate, otherwise unconditional, moral principles.

Does this mean that necessity never confers permission to resort to special measures in the face of necessity? Does this mean, for example, that the state cannot sacrifice transparency and accountability when secrecy is necessary to national security? This does not follow, but to see this we have to let go of the idea that necessity-driven infringements of fundamental moral norms can be seen as acts permissible under moral rules. Harel and Sharon distinguish between principled and unprincipled acts. This distinction is familiar from the dirty hands and just war literatures. In these contexts, scholars recognize that circumstances can make violations of moral principles by political actors necessary and therefore permissible but claim that such necessary violations are not permissible by some competing moral norm or principle. As Harel and Sharon rephrase this position:

> Violations of our most fundamental norms may be unavoidable. But – and this is the crucial point – this does not entail a rejection or modification of our basic rules. What allows the [violation] is solely the necessity of avoiding catastrophe, not a different law allowing [violation] under some conditions.[45]

Their position claims that moral principles know no exceptions; it concedes, however, that there may be exceptional cases beyond moral principles. In terms of practical reasoning, this means that the political agent violating moral principles is not governed by a moral principle permitting the violation under exceptional circumstances (even if it is correct to say that the agent violating a moral principle is governed by that moral principle in the sense that she decides to go against it, nonetheless the "when" and the "why" of its violation is not so governed). In effect, even if she believes that violation under these circumstances is morally required and that in similar cases such violations are necessary, when the new circumstances materialize she has to reconsider the circumstances afresh and make a new decision.[46] As Harel and Sharon explain, necessary violations are permitted as "singular act[s], particular to the case at hand and not a generalizable norm that may be used in guiding future decisions."[47]

The argument that necessary violations remain morally unlegislatable has clear implications for the question of the state's authority to resort to special measures, including secrecy. Given that (a) the political authority of the state, as contrary to an arbitrary exercise of power, is founded on moral principles and subject to corresponding constraints,[48] and (b) necessity-driven departures from fundamental moral norms, *pace* threshold deontology, resist framing in terms of moral principles, necessity cannot ground the political authority of the state to violate fundamental moral norms. Acts of violation of fundamental moral norms can be performed strictly from the necessity of the circumstances and not as a matter of authorized state policy.

This argument lays bare some of the problems involved in the seminal defense of state secrecy as proposed by Amy Gutmann and Dennis Thompson and developed in Thompson's subsequent work.[49] While they deny that the direct appeals to the necessity of secrecy by the executive suffice to make secrecy legitimate, they admit that necessary secrets can be legitimate if their necessity is acknowledged by citizens: "The secrecy is justified not only because it is necessary for the policy, but also because the question of whether and in what form it is necessary is itself the subject of public deliberation."[50] Making the necessity of secrecy the subject of public deliberation does not require that the executive disclose secret policies; it only requires that the executive admit that they resort to secrecy and indicate the reasons for this even though they do not disclose the specific contents of the secret policies and processes. According to Gutmann and Thompson, such "second-order publicity about first-order secrecy"[51] enables citizens to publicly deliberate about the necessity for secrecy and, at least partly, to authorize it. Thompson acknowledged that the limited scope of information revealed by the executive may be insufficient for an act of authorization to be valid.[52] Even if such problems could be mitigated, however, this argument fails to authorize the state's appeals to necessity for reasons indicated earlier: necessity-driven special measures cannot be seen as exercises of authority because appeals to necessity escape the normative codification that the concept of authority presupposes.

If necessity does not authorize states to resort to special measures violating otherwise fundamental moral and legal principles even if it may permit them to do so, how should we conceptualize the permissibility at issue? The concept of "vindication" introduced by David Owen is helpful to mark the difference between the kind of permissibility to act at stake here and the one involved in being authorized to act in that way.[53] The concept of (political) authority refers to justificatory reasons that can be given independently and in advance of the action; in this sense (political) authority is always prospective. Vindication comes into play when justificatory reasons cannot be given independently and in advance of the action in question, but the agents do not have reasons, all things considered, to regret having performed it despite the moral costs it involved; in this sense, vindication is retrospective. Importantly, Owen emphasizes, vindication does not "retrospectively justify"[54] acts that violate moral principles. Such actions remain morally unjustified, but their performance is vindicated by the value it has brought about. Owen associates vindication with the kind of permissibility pertaining to morally unjustified action the performance of which turned out to be necessary for the establishment of good ends as in Machiavelli's doctrine of reason of state. In his view, the concept of vindication also makes sense of a common reaction to political actors whose hands are dirty: We realize that their action was morally wrong but are glad that they did what they did.[55] Applying this concept to special measures adopted by the state in the face of necessity, we can say that while not authorized, they may nonetheless be vindicated insofar as the political community would have reason, all things considered, not to regret the introduction of special measures despite the moral costs involved.

Against my conclusion that necessity cannot ground political authority to resort to special measures such as secrecy because necessity escapes any normative codification that the concept of political authority presupposes, the following objection can be raised. The argument above concedes that there are circumstances in which agents can be vindicated in infringing otherwise unconditional moral principles. If so, then agents can be called upon to do so when these circumstances obtain. It follows that agents should identify whether exceptional circumstances obtain or not. For this purpose, they should construct a rule identifying exceptional circumstances. Insofar as the argument above must be committed to admit that such a rule can be constructed and acted on, its insistence that necessity considerations escape normative codification and, as such, cannot ground political authority to violate fundamental moral norms is unfounded.[56]

This objection posits that there must be a rule specifying what is to count as exceptional circumstances. Yet, as Harel and Sharon retort, there cannot be a rule specifying what is to count as exceptional circumstances because then these circumstances would not be exceptional. Moreover, in claiming that a rule is required in order to determine whether standard moral rules apply (normal circumstances) or not (exceptional circumstances), the objection lapses into a vicious regress: if in order to determine whether a standard moral rule holds we must refer to another rule, we must be able to verify the validity of that other rule. Given that we can do that only by reference to yet another rule, the problem re-appears at this (and every subsequent) level as well. As an attempt to reinstate the idea of moral rules permitting violation of moral rules, this objection fails.

The question addressed in this chapter is whether in a situation of necessity, a resort to secrecy (or other special measures that override the moral and legal constraints that normally apply to political action) is a legitimate exercise of political authority vested in liberal-democratic states. Having discussed this from the perspective of moral theory, my answer is negative: necessity does not confer political authority on the state to deploy special measures, including secrecy, because necessity escapes the normative codification that the idea of political authority presupposes. Hence, to return to the examples opening my chapter, the appeals to the necessity of secrecy, which motivated the UK government's refusal to disclose Cabinet minutes in which British involvement in the Iraq war was deliberated, and similar appeals that motivated the Polish government's refusal to confirm or deny its involvement in the CIA extraordinary rendition program are insufficient to render executive secrecy in these cases legitimate. In the next section, I consider the question whether in a situation of necessity, a resort to secrecy is a legitimate exercise of political authority vested in liberal-democratic states from the perspective of jurisprudence.

3.7 Necessity escapes legal codification

In early modernity, lawyers would place the special powers claimed by government in situations of necessity within the sphere of the prerogative, a power to be exercised in the public good that operates outside and against the existing framework of standing laws.[57] Nowadays, as Giorgio Agamben observes, the idea that special powers that empower government beyond their usual mandate could be extra-legal is rejected.[58] One believes that necessity-driven departures from the law can be accommodated in the legal system. We can legally suspend the law by creating "carve-outs" into law that specify circumstances in which it can be suspended. For example, law protects freedom of expression defined as the right to receive information and ideas without interference by public authorities but, at the same time, it allows states to derogate from it during a state of emergency; thus, transparency legislation creates exemption clauses that recognize that there are circumstances under which information should not be released. Similarly, law protects freedom of assembly, freedom of thought, conscience, and religion but allows states to suspend these freedoms during a state of emergency.

There are two main strategies to accommodate the special measures the state adopts to respond to a necessity in the legal framework of liberal-democratic states. The first proposes to subject them to *ex ante* constitutional provisions: special emergency provisions are added to the constitution for regulating and constraining departures from law adopted by the state in situations of necessity. This model is adopted in a majority of the legal frameworks of liberal-democratic states.[59]

The second approach subjects special powers to ordinary law regulation and ongoing or *ex post* juridical or parliamentary oversight. Unlike emergency constitutions, which specify the substantive conditions of necessity prior to any particular event, ordinary legislation grants power to the executive when a crisis is expected or has already presented itself. This is done either through the adoption of new legislation that grants the government special powers or through the reinterpretation of existing law. This model enables the legislature to stay in control, allowing it (instead of the constitution) to decide when a situation calls for special measures and which powers to hand over to the executive to address it. The legislature and the courts are also expected to monitor the use of the special powers, to investigate abuses, to extend these powers if necessary, and to suspend them if the emergency ends.

To the extent that the law claims to regulate and constrain the special measures the state adopts in situations of necessity, secrecy appears to be a legitimate tool for the exercise of political authority in liberal-democratic states. Indeed, political actors often see it this way. As Dorothee Riese's research reveals, the idea that legal regulation confers legitimacy on the executive's appeals to necessity prevailed in recent debates in the German Bundestag on granting intelligence agencies extraordinary powers in the context of security policies. MPs agreed that intelligence secrecy was justified insofar as it was necessary. As in reason of state thinking, they believed that necessity trumped the moral and legal principles underpinning the liberal-democratic order, such as protection of individual rights or transparency. Despite the democratic deficits of this course of action, they considered the executive's appeals to necessity legitimate as long as they were legally regulated. In pushing for legal enclosure of necessary secrecy, Riese claims, "German parliamentary practice can be seen as an attempt at democratizing . . . the idea of reason of state which otherwise is often considered as . . . inherently anti-democratic."[60]

How successful this strategy to accommodate the special powers of the state in the legal framework of the liberal-democratic state is has been the subject of an extensive discussion in jurisprudence. The objections raised against both proposals revolve around the difficulty of codifying the requirements of necessity. Mark Tushnet points out that prospectively codifying, let alone constraining, special measures called for in a situation of necessity is impossible.[61] Legislators cannot predict what crisis situations may arise and what special measures might be necessary to manage them. In addition, with regard to any codification in place, necessity could be invoked to override them. To illustrate this, Tushnet asks us first to list the circumstances that would justify the suspension of legality in the face of emergency and then to imagine that a new emergency arises that the list failed to foresee. In such cases, the government can claim that:

> [T]he emergency is so pressing that it requires suspension of the legality expressed in the list of criteria for determining whether legality should be suspended, and the procedures for doing so. There is no response to this argument available to those who believe that suspension of legality is sometimes defensible.[62]

Just as ordinary legislation, emergency legislation must also be subject to suspension should the executive deem this necessary.

The conceptual difficulty of codifying the necessity of secrecy and other special powers the executive may adopt in order to avert the threats to political survival and government's capacity for action bears on the character of many existing constitutional emergency clauses. William Scheuerman observes that these provisions pay less attention to providing prospectively a substantive definition of what specific events deserve to be described as a "necessity" and, instead, focus on establishing procedural mechanisms of delegating and overseeing special powers, leaving it largely to the executive actors to determine whether or not a particular development constitutes a necessity situation and what measures are needed to address it.[63] Yet if the judgments about necessity are for the executive to make, then legal provisions do not function as constraints on its action but rather as factors about which the executive will decide. In effect, they permit government to do as it pleases while claiming to act within its legitimate authority. As Tushnet argues, "The provisions provide executive officials with a fig leaf of legal justification for the expansive use of sheer power. What appears to be emergency power limited by the rule of law is actually unlimited emergency power."[64]

Similar problems confront the model that seeks to legalize special executive powers through ordinary law. Here, when adopting new legislation in the face of an emergency, legislators tend to codify the discretionary powers of the executive in a vague and open-ended way in order to ensure that the government enjoys all the powers needed to deal with the crisis at hand. Or, when interpreting existing law, they adopt extremely expansive readings of their statutory and constitutional powers, on the one hand, and very narrow readings of existing laws that might otherwise constrain their behavior, on the other. The legal justification of even the most controversial measures the US government adopted in the "war on terror" provides an apt example of inventive interpretation of existing law, as Clement Fatovic and Benjamin Kleinerman argue: lawyers working in the Office of Legal Counsel claimed legal authority for torture and the targeted assassination of American citizens and foreign nationals suspected of waging war against the United States and maintained that the Geneva Conventions of 1949 and other domestic and international law do not apply to these measures.[65]

These concerns illustrate that seeking legal authority for even the most controversial actions the executive takes in the face of necessity commits us to accepting a situation in which, despite the facade of legality, there is illegality or, in David Dyzenhaus' words "an absence of law prescribed by law under the concept of necessity."[66] While defenders of the second model reserve an important role for judges in overseeing the executive's deployment of special powers and making sure that it observes the basic values of the rule of law, legal practice shows that judges defer to the executive in times of crisis. Eric Posner and Adrian Vermeule point out that laying the judgment of the legitimacy of executive action in their hands would be unworkable: deciding what qualifies as a situation of necessity and what would be the most appropriate response is a matter of political judgment that goes beyond their competence; to have them do this would be to require them to second guess the judgment of the executive.[67]

The problem with legal codification of necessity-driven exemptions to law is that it inherently involves the possibility of its own suspension. The law says nothing more than "the executive shall have the right to do whatever it pleases," in which case the law becomes meaningless as a constraint on the special measures the executive adopts, as Fatovic and Kleinerman have shown.[68] Unlimited power of this kind is in tension with the concept of legal authority. To the extent that authority is constrained by norms that legitimate it, legal authority to resort to special measures that resist any legal codification is difficult to defend. I conclude that the attempts to confer legal authority upon the executive to resort to special measures overriding legal and moral principles that normally constrain political action fail. This conclusion aligns with the work of those legal scholars who, like Tushnet, Dyzenhaus, and Oren Gross, oppose the incorporation of special measures into the legal system. As I have shown, there is a deeper layer to the problem with emergency powers they identified: their argument restates, in juridical terms, the problem we encountered when exploring the political authority of the state to resort to special powers. There it turned out to be difficult, on pain of falling prey to slippery-slope reasoning, to determine the necessity threshold at which the state could exercise political authority to violate moral constraints that otherwise apply to its action. Here it turns out to be difficult to legally codify special powers of the state to violate law. In both contexts, in the absence of such constraints, the prospect of unlimited power looms large.

Doubts about the legitimacy of special measures adopted by the state in situations of necessity spill over into doubts about the status of jurisdiction in related areas, such as whistleblowing. The US Whistleblower Protection Act grants the president authority to exempt any positions from its protection when the president finds it "necessary and warranted by conditions of good administration."[69] Given the inherently open-ended and unrestricted character of necessity and the court's deference to the executive, this leaves government whistleblowers unprotected. This outcome has struck activists and legal scholars as problematic, sparking a discussion on the justification of whistleblowing and the need to revise whistleblowing protection legislation.[70]

If the state has no legal authority to resort to special measures that violate moral and legal principles that otherwise underpin political order, does it mean that the state is never permitted to resort to special measures, including secrecy, prompted by their necessity? Some contemporary jurists who oppose the incorporation of special measures into legal rules, for example, Gross, Tushnet, and David Feldman, postulate allowing for emergency measures while conceptualizing them as external to the legal authority of the state.[71] In this, they echo the claim that even though the state does not exercise authority when resorting to special measures, it may be vindicated in doing so. Yet if special measures cannot be accommodated in the legal framework and thus authorized, it remains unclear what expression such vindication could take. Some advocates of the extra-legality of special measures, such as Harel and Sharon, propose that the courts could exempt public officials from responsibility or grant *ex-post* exemption. Such *ex-post* exemption may be facilitated by prosecutorial discretion, pardoning, or other tools that highlight the exceptional and unprincipled nature of the circumstances giving rise to the act.[72] Gross and Feldman propose another mechanism. Since the issue concerns whether the people have reason, all things considered, to affirm the actions undertaken by the government, then some process for determining that seems to be required. Thus, they advocate subjecting extra-legal emergency action to public judgment *ex post,* which might excuse the illegal action or even effectively endorse it by more conventional political mechanisms.[73] Yet another mechanism could be a trial by citizen assembly, which could reach a judgment *ex ante*. For example, if a government perceives a situation as one of necessity and believes that it would be best to engage in democratically unjustified action, they set up a citizen's assembly to deliberate *in camera* on (a) whether the situation is one of necessity, (b) whether the proposed course of action could be vindicated by any outcome, and (c) what the requirements of vindication would be. This could serve as a democratic mechanism for vindicating immoral actions under conditions that are legitimately considered situations of necessity.[74]

3.8 Conclusion

From the claim that secrecy is a necessary condition of the political survival of a democratic state and/or the capacity for action of a democratic government, proponents of the necessity-based defense of state secrecy infer that secrecy is a legitimate exercise of democratic authority. This chapter concludes, however, that an appeal to its necessity fails to ground the authority of executive secrecy, even if it can vindicate it. Necessity cannot ground its authority because it escapes normative codification in both the moral and legal domains. As no moral or legal norm can fully capture and constrain special measures adopted by the state in the face of necessity, such measures open the door to unlimited executive powers operating in a discretionary space of action impenetrable to democratic scrutiny. In light of this, the necessity argument fails in escaping the anti-democratic implications of reason of state thinking. Necessary secrets, contrary to what proponents of the necessity argument claim, are not a legitimate form of democratic governance, but at most its vindicated suspension.

The overall conclusion of the chapter, however, is not that secrecy, along with other special measures the state adopts in situations of necessity, is illegitimate but only that an appeal to necessity does not suffice to legitimate them. An account of the democratic authority of state secrecy must proceed in terms other than their necessity.

Notes

1 This chapter draws from Mokrosinska 2022.
2 Grieve 2012, 3–4.
3 Gasztold 2022.
4 Miller, Press Conference 2014, quoted in Gasztold 2022, 317.
5 Roberts 2006(b).
6 Fabre 2022.
7 Fabre 2022, 4.
8 Davis Cross 2018, 916.
9 Buzan, Wæver and de Wilde 1998.
10 Rittberger and Goetz 2018, 3.
11 Neocleus 2000, 10.
12 Dijstelbloem and Pelizza 2019.
13 Thompson 1999, 182.
14 Stiglitz 2002, 36.
15 Thompson 1999, 185.
16 Warren and Mansbridge 2016; Lee 2019. For a discussion of the impact of publicity on the quality of decision-making, see Chapter 6, sec. 2.
17 Aldrich and Richterova 2018, 1006.

18 Boot 2019(a), 496.
19 Plotke 1997; Urbinati 2006; Christiano 1996, ch. 3.
20 Rosenblum 2005, 147.
21 Machiavelli 1950.
22 For a historical overview of the place of secrecy in the reason of state doctrine, see Bodei 2011.
23 Meinecke 1998, 1, 3.
24 Schmitt 2005, ch. 1.
25 Fabre 2022, 47.
26 Schoenfeld 2010, 21.
27 Schoenfeld 2010, ch. 7.
28 Rittberger and Goetz 2018, 7.
29 Scheffler 1988, 1.
30 For a consequentialist defense of special state powers (torture), see Seidman 2005.
31 This view is inspired by Kant, whose "On the Alleged Right to Lie from Philanthropy" is regarded as its paradigmatic expression, Kant 1996.
32 Compare Harel and Sharon's discussion on the deontological and consequentialist assessment of the state's special powers to resort to torture (2011, 847).
33 See Kagan 1988, 78–94.
34 Fabre 2022, 30.
35 Harel and Sharon 2011, 851.
36 Harel and Sharon 2011.
37 Cf. Ripstein 2004, 34. See also Besson 2014.
38 Sagar 2013, 111.
39 Fenster 2017, 176.
40 MOJ 2012.
41 Graham 2012. Cf. Thomas 2020.
42 Waldron 2005, 1741.
43 Harel and Sharon 2011.
44 Aquinas 1999, v. 2 q 96, art 6. The Kantian version of the argument is that by incorporating exceptions to moral laws, one undermines their status as moral laws: "exceptions would nullify the universality on account of which alone they are called principles" (Kant 1996, 6: 221).
45 Harel and Sharon 2011, 863.
46 Harel and Sharon 2008, 251, n. 29.
47 Harel and Sharon 2008, 252.
48 For an overview of recent discussions of political authority, see Wendt 2019.
49 Gutmann and Thompson 1996; Thompson 1999.
50 Gutmann and Thompson 1996, 103–104.
51 Thompson 1999, 185.
52 Thompson 1987, 23–24.
53 Owen 2020.
54 Owen 2020, 160.
55 Owen 2020, 161.
56 Harel and Sharon 2011, 860–861.
57 Poole 2016, 149; Locke 1988, ch. 14.
58 Agamben 2005, 25.
59 For an overview and analysis of emergency legal frameworks, see Ferejohn and Pasquino 2004.
60 Riese 2020, 166.
61 Tushnet 2005, 43. The point initially made by Schmitt 2005, 13.
62 Tushnet 2005, 47.
63 Scheuerman 2006, 66.

64 Tushnet 2005, 48–49.
65 Fatovic and Kleinerman 2013, 3.
66 Dyzenhaus 2012, 447.
67 Posner and Vermeule 2010, 53.
68 Fatovic and Kleinerman 2013, 7.
69 Fenster 2017, 89.
70 Benkler 2014; Boot 2019(b); PEN American Center 2015, 9.
71 Tushnet 2005; Gross 2003; Feldman 2008.
72 Harel and Sharon 2008, 258–259.
73 Gross 2003, 1099; Feldman 2008, 565.
74 I thank David Owen for this suggestion.

4 Do states have a right to privacy?

4.1 Introduction

According to the necessity argument discussed in the previous chapter, states may legitimately restrict access to government information insofar as the restrictions are necessary to secure their basic interests. "Necessity" marks a tipping point at which the positive effects of the state's withholding of information outweigh countervailing considerations. The argument discussed in this chapter preserves the idea that withholding information may be necessary but gives it a conceptual makeover.[1] While the state's claim to restrict access is presented as necessary, it is detached from a cost-benefit calculus and asserted to be a matter of the state's rights *viz.* its right to privacy.[2] What brings this argument close to the necessity argument is the idea that privacy, in the words of the doyen of liberal privacy scholarship Alan Westin, is a "functional necessity."[3] The lack of privacy compromises the autonomy and integrity of political decision-making. Unlike the necessity argument, however, proponents of this argument claim that the state's restrictions on access are permitted not in virtue of the positive consequences they bring about (or the negative consequences they avert) but because they are expressions of the rights states exercise as autonomous agents.

The argument defending the state's right to privacy emerged in the late 1960s and 1970s in the writings of liberal privacy scholars Alan Westin and Edward Bloustein.[4] It had not had much purchase in mainstream privacy discourse and in (inter)national jurisdiction until it re-emerged in the debate on unauthorized disclosures of classified government information sparked by WikiLeaks' and Snowden's disclosures. Andrew Murray, the legal scholar who revived Westin's defense of the state's right to privacy, claimed that WikiLeaks and Snowden, by disclosing classified information concerning intelligence programs, military operations, or diplomatic cables, violated the privacy of states to which the disclosed information referred.[5]

According to Murray, states, just like individuals, have a right to privacy that protects their capacity for autonomous action *viz.* their capacity to formulate and act on their (organizational) goals. Just as individuals have a right

DOI: 10.4324/9781003083733-4

to conduct their affairs without having to keep up a public face, so also "the government," he argues echoing Westin, "requires periods where it can find release from the constant scrutiny of its public role."[6] In Westin's view, states, by virtue of their right to privacy, are entitled to keep certain economic and law enforcement policies, diplomacy, intelligence, and defense programs out of the view of citizens and the media. They are also entitled to conduct decision-making processes behind closed doors.[7] Murray places particular emphasis on the part of Westin's argument that deals with the private character of internal communications between state officials: on this argument, internal memos, minutes of proceedings, voting records, policy discussions, and political bargaining, especially in the early stages of policy formulation, are a matter of state privacy. He writes:

> WikiLeaks is bad for democracy. With the changes to society brought about by the rise of the information society and sites like WikiLeaks, we may now not be affording the necessary level of privacy protection to decision-makers to carry out this staging process [of policy formulation].[8]

The value of privacy is acknowledged in both liberal and democratic political thoughts and, thus, if Murray's argument is successful, it will provide an interesting liberal-democratic defense of the state's claim to withhold information from citizens. Is it successful?

I begin my discussion in Section 4.2, by considering a general objection to the idea that states have a right to privacy. According to the objection, rights pertain to individuals only: groups, including states, cannot exercise rights, privacy, or otherwise.[9] In response to this objection, I claim that rights to group privacy may be defended and that we may grant privacy to, for example, private clubs, institutions, business corporations, or juries. In Section 4.3, I focus on governments and parliaments as instances of groups and argue, in Section 4.4, that even if they are organized groups, they are not the kind of groups that may exercise a right to privacy against citizens. This is because (a) democratic governance involves mechanisms of accountability whereas (b) privacy rights, by their nature, are rights to not be held accountable within the domain they protect. Judith DeCew put it aptly when she defined privacy as "a property of types of information and activity viewed . . . as beyond the legitimate concern of others."[10] Thus, conceiving the state's claim to restrict access in terms of its right to privacy would place classified information, secret policies, and processes beyond political accountability. This, in turn, just as in the case of the necessity defense of state secrecy, would make it hard to set effective constraints on the state's action. In Section 4.5, I briefly compare the normative properties of privacy and secrecy and conclude, in Section 4.6, that while democratic states cannot have a right to privacy, it remains an open question whether they can have a right to resort to secrecy.

4.2 Group privacy

Privacy, Westin says, is "the claim of individuals, groups, or institutions to determine for themselves when, how, and to what extent information about them is communicated to others."[11] Among groups having a right to privacy, Westin lists families, corporations, trade unions, universities, churches, hospitals, welfare organizations, civic groups, political parties, and courts. Importantly, he also lists governments and parliaments.[12] It is this argument presenting state privacy as a species of group privacy that Murray sets out to revive.

Westin and Murray define privacy as the control that agents, both individuals and groups, have over access to themselves.[13] Privacy so understood has an informational and a decisional dimension. Informational privacy refers to control over access to information about agents: it entitles individuals and groups to withhold their data from others' scrutiny. Decisional privacy refers to the control that individuals and groups have over their ability to engage in certain types of action: it removes their choices and actions from interference by others.

Privacy as control over access does not refer to the physical power to grant or deny access. It is about normative control involving a moral claim on the part of the agents to limit the liberty of anyone else to search for information or to interfere with their decisions. In this normative sense, privacy is a right that imposes correlated duties on other parties to refrain from seeking access to the material that is withheld from them.

To defend a right to privacy on the part of individuals and groups, one has to present them as agents capable of bearing rights. What kind of capacity must the agent possess to be capable of bearing rights? Two competing theories have dominated the discussion on this issue: the choice theory and the interest theory of rights. According to choice theory, rights provide normative protection for the exercise of autonomous choices.[14] On this theory, for a group to be a right-holder, it must be an agent with a capacity for autonomous choice. According to the interest theory of rights, rights protect certain kinds of interests. From this perspective, for a group to be a right-holder, it must be an agent with a capacity for having appropriate interests, for example, well-being. Westin understands a right to privacy as a shield protecting the capacity for autonomous action. This view commits him to the choice theory of rights and to seeing groups as agents with the capacity for autonomous choice.

In linking a right to privacy to autonomy, Westin focuses first on individuals and subsequently extends his argument to groups. Autonomy, in its generic sense, means self-government. Individuals are self-governing if they live their lives according to reasons which are their own and not the product of manipulative or distorting forces external to them. The right to informational and decisional privacy protects individuals' autonomy so understood because it endows them with normative powers to determine what others may or may not do to them: what information about them others may or may not access and whether or not they may interfere with their choices. It is in virtue of this normative control that individuals are allowed to remove themselves from their social environment thus minimizing the chances of external interference and manipulation. Hence, Westin conceptualized privacy as the right to "voluntary and temporary withdrawal . . . from the general society."[15] The right to privacy as the right to control access corresponds to duties on the part of others to refrain from scrutiny and interference within the domain protected by privacy. In this sense, privacy carves out a space around individuals in which they can direct their lives as they see fit, independently of social and political pressures.

Westin extends this argument to groups. Groups exercise group autonomy if they formulate and pursue their group goals free from external interference and manipulation. Westin calls this "organizational" autonomy.[16] Group privacy protects the organizational autonomy of groups because it allows them to control what information about them non-members may or may not access and whether or not they may interfere with their group decisions. This normative control corresponds to the duties group privacy imposes upon non-members to refrain from seeking information that the group withholds and refrain from interference with its decisions. In this way, privacy makes it possible for groups to remove themselves from their social environment thus minimizing their exposure to external scrutiny, interference, and manipulation. The importance of privacy on the part of groups, including states, reflects, for Westin, the imperative of privacy on the part of individuals:

> Just as individuals need privacy to evaluate what is happening to them and to decide how to respond, so organizations need privacy to plan their courses of action. . . . The lack of privacy . . . can threaten the independence or autonomous life of an organization.[17]

Before I proceed, one qualification. In the individual case, having autonomy seems sufficient for granting a person a right to privacy. It is not clear, however, whether Westin would present autonomy as a sufficient condition of the right to privacy on the part of organizations. Possibly, he would agree that there are organizations that should not exist, and should have no rights, but which possess autonomy (e.g., the Mafia). In this case, the organization's capacity for autonomy is a condition of its right to privacy unless it engages in immoral actions. Autonomy and the moral permissibility of actions are, then, each a necessary condition and are only jointly sufficient for a right to privacy on the part of organizations.

In extending the right of privacy to groups, Westin assumes that groups are autonomous agents capable of bearing rights. Unlike the case of individuals, presenting groups as agents capable of bearing rights encounters two objections.

4.2.1 First objection: groups are not (autonomous) agents

Pace Westin, the idea that groups are autonomous agents has been contested. One objection targets the ontological status of groups calling into question the existence of groups as entities that have properties that are not the mere aggregation of properties of the individuals making them up. If groups do not exist, the question of whether they can be seen as autonomous agents is answered in the negative. Answering skepticism about the ontological status of groups in a satisfactory way would require engaging with the work on group agency in the field of social ontology.[18] As this would take us beyond the scope of this chapter, let me only indicate the line of reasoning most charitable to the argument that states, along with other groups, have a right to privacy.

Reflecting on the debate whether and in what sense groups can be agents capable of bearing rights, Luciano Floridi points out that we can have clear cases in which members of a group have properties that the set they make up does not. For example, Floridi argues that a pile of books does not have some properties that single book-members of the pile-set have: single books have an author, a pile of books does not. But reverse cases are equally possible. For example, a pile of books has the property of being "too heavy to be moved by a single person" even though none of the books comprising the pile has this property.[19] Another example of a property of a group/set that is not a property of its members is the number of members of the set.[20] Drawing on these examples, one can claim that it is possible for groups to exist in the sense in which it is possible for a group/set to have properties that are not properties of its individual members/tokens.

Assuming that groups exist, a next challenge is to argue that they can be seen as autonomous agents, which is a condition of their being (privacy) right-holders. An important objection to the idea that groups can be autonomous agents runs as follows: if a necessary condition of autonomy is a capacity to choose and act on one's own reasons, then groups are not autonomous agents because groups have no reasons of their own. More generally, groups have no mental states that would make them capable of intentional choice and action. Whatever beliefs, desires, and intentions groups have, they are reducible to the beliefs, desires, and intentions of their individual members. Whatever reasons groups have, these reasons are reducible to the reasons of individual group members.[21] The implication of this position for the status of groups as holders of privacy rights is clear: if groups have no capacity for autonomous choice and action, then they cannot be right-holders; if groups cannot be right-holders, they cannot hold a right to privacy either.

Obviously, not every collection of individuals can be considered as a group capable of autonomous choice and action. Scholars argue that some threshold of unity and self-awareness as a group among members has to be reached. This may reflect, for example, collective identity that survives changes in individual membership, collective goals, and intentional coordination toward reaching them. These properties, in turn, presuppose (formalized) decision-making procedures.[22] The existence of decision-making procedures would then mark groups as autonomous agents capable of exercising rights. Wayne Sumner has aptly articulated this idea:

> [T]he capacity for agency is a logical pre-condition of having rights. But every social group which qualifies as either an institution or an association must have some procedure of reaching collective decisions and taking collective action. . . . Collectivities will qualify as the subjects of rights as long as they possess the requisite capacity to act on behalf of their members.[23]

Sumner is right to indicate that outcomes of collective decision-making mechanisms count as group decisions. However, it is fair to ask whether the reasons such collective decisions provide are sufficiently distinct from their individual components in order to conceive of a group as an autonomous agent. In response to this challenge, Philip Pettit demonstrates that the only way in which a collection of individuals can arrive at a consistent decision is by allowing decision-making rules that "break on some issues with the judgments of a majority, perhaps even a unanimity, of its members,"[24] that is, lead individuals to adopt a decision at the group level that does not reproduce the judgment of the majority. Leaving aside the social choice theory details of this argument,[25] let me indicate its implications. In demonstrating that the only method of arriving at a collective decision is by adopting those collective decision-making mechanisms that will allow for a situation in which group judgments and individual judgments come apart, Pettit implies that the outcomes of collective decision-making do not collapse into individual components and, thus, are sufficiently distinct from them to conceive of a group as forming and acting on its own reasons. Following this line of argument, he defends the idea that groups are autonomous agents in the sense that they have reasons that are not reducible to the reasons of their individual members. As he puts it, groups – "companies, churches, courts, and cabinets"[26] – have their own minds.

If we accept the argument that groups are capable of forming and acting on their own group reason, then it makes sense, I submit, to speak of rights protecting its exercise. It thus makes sense to speak of a group right of privacy as Westin does. A group right of privacy ensures that the "group mind" operates without external interference and manipulation insofar as it confers normative powers upon a group to exercise control over what other agents may do: the degree to which they ought to refrain from information access about the group in question and interference with its choices.

4.2.2 Second objection: group privacy is reducible to the privacies of individual group members

Whereas the first concern about group privacy dealt with the question of whether groups can be autonomous agents capable of bearing rights, the other concern is that group privacy is merely a misleading way to talk about the privacies of individual group members, taken together. Taking issue with Westin's argument that "claims to privacy given to organizations . . . are more than a protection of the collective privacy rights of the members as individuals,"[27] the objection is that group privacy collapses into the aggregated privacies of individual group members and, hence, has no distinct normative status from individual privacy. The challenge facing proponents of group privacy is then to demonstrate that privacy as a group right belongs only to a group, not to a group insofar as it is constituted by individual members who have this right.

For a start, one could conceptualize group privacy rights on the model of Floridi's example of a pile of books referred to earlier. One could say that group privacy is a property of a group and not a property of the group members in the same sense in which the property of "being too heavy to carry" is a property of a pile of books and not of the individual books that make it up. As Floridi observes, there are rights that meet this description. For example, a right to national self-determination is a property of a group but not of its members in the sense that it is held by a nation as a whole and not by its members individually.[28] In order to substantiate the idea of group privacy as a property distinct from individual privacies (or the sum thereof), Floridi provides the following example:

> Consider . . . the case in which the close friends and relatives (the group) of a deceased person decide to hold a private funeral. Attendance is by invitation only, but this is not meant to make the funeral 'exclusive'. The desired privacy may be due to a need for intimacy . . . or perhaps because of cultural or religious customs. Whatever the reasons, in this case it seems very counterintuitive to argue that each member of the group (each close friend or relative of the deceased) has a right to a private funeral, or that the privacy demanded is just the collection of all individual privacies. It seems more reasonable to admit that . . . [i]t is the whole group as a group that has a right to that specific kind of privacy.[29]

These arguments do not eliminate all concerns of the critics. Imagine that an intruder shows up infringing the group's right to privacy in Floridi's example. Would it not be the case that the group members, and not merely the group, suffer the loss of privacy? If this is the case, then this demonstrates that to the extent that we can speak of group rights to privacy, these rights are never held exclusively by groups but always also by their individual members.

In response to this concern, Steven Davis has offered a thought experiment meant to illustrate that a violation of group privacy need not involve a violation of privacy of the individual members of the group and, thus, group privacy is not reducible to the privacies of individual group members. He asks us to imagine a

> society that has rituals, information about which the society wishes to keep from the public eye. If the rituals of the group were reported in the newspaper, but no names of members were reported, the group could claim that it had suffered a loss of its privacy, but no member could claim such a loss.[30]

As presented in the thought experiment, the disclosure of confidential information at hand is a violation of privacy. However, even though the disclosure violates privacy, we cannot point to any particular individual group member whose privacy has been violated: as they remain anonymous, their privacy has been retained. This thought experiment shows that a group can experience a loss of privacy independently of any loss of privacy on the part of its individual members. To say that a group can lose privacy even if none of its members loses her privacy is to say that group privacy is not reducible to individual privacy but has its own normative standing.

Against that argument, proponents of the reductionist argument could raise the following objection: it is usual for individual members personally to identify themselves with the group and consider information about the group to be information about themselves. If that is the case, then, when information about the group is being disclosed, information about its individual members is also being disclosed. In effect, when a group loses its privacy, individual group members also lose their privacy. Hence, group privacy can be spelled out in terms of the individual privacies of the group members. In response, I admit that this argument, if correct, demonstrates that group privacy is linked to individual privacy. I deny, however, that the link between group privacy and the individual privacy it presupposes reduces group privacy to the privacies of its individual members. Travis Dumsday rightly observes that if the individual were not a member of the group, she would not be implicated in the group privacy loss, and, thus, according to this argument, it is the loss of privacy on the part of the group that causes the loss of privacy on the part of its members. To say that it is the loss of privacy on the part of the group that causes the loss of privacy on the part of its members "has the result that group privacy is just as real as individual privacy and cannot be reduced to the latter, since it causes the latter in such cases. For reduction to be possible, the dependence would have to flow in the opposite direction."[31]

The thrust of my discussion above is that we have sufficient reason to accept Westin's claim that groups are autonomous agents, who by virtue of their autonomy are capable of bearing a right to privacy against non-members (unless they engage in immoral actions). If we indeed accept this claim, does that imply that governments and parliaments have a right to privacy?

4.3 From group privacy to state privacy

Governments and parliaments are instances of groups, hence, by a simple extension of the argument, governments and parliaments would have rights to privacy (unless they engage, like the Mafia, in immoral actions). Along the lines of Westin's argument, they would hold a right to privacy by virtue of their organizational autonomy, that is, their capacity to formulate and act on their organizational goals. Westin coins the term "executive privacy" to refer to the government's privacy.[32] "Legislative privacy" is the term Bloustein coins to refer to group privacy on the part of legislative bodies.[33]

What would be the object of executive and legislative privacy? If privacy protects a group's autonomy, then, endorsing Pettit's understanding of group autonomy, we could say that privacy protects the capacity of the group to formulate and act on its own group reason. With regard to governments and parliaments, then, privacy would protect their group reason formation: (1) the process through which officials and representatives formulate their individual judgments and (2) the collective decision processes that transform their individual judgments into a political decision, law, or policy. Privacy would protect the decision-making process by cutting it off from the external environment and thereby minimize the risk of external manipulation and interference.

Without privacy protection, one might worry, the formation of group reason and, thus, group autonomy, might be disrupted. Of particular concern for Westin is the impact of the exposure of decision-making processes on the incentives and quality of arguments that decision-makers employ. Thus, he points out that exposing communications between decision-makers might make them conform their individual judgments to the undue pressure of various external interest groups. In isolating decision-makers from interference and manipulation by external lobby groups, privacy preserves the autonomy of their decision-making process. Just like proponents of the necessity argument, Westin sees closed-door deliberation and decision-making settings as a necessary condition of government's capacity for decision and action: "Privacy in governmental decision-making is a functional necessity for the formulation of responsible policy."[34]

In current political practice, one can encounter arguments that emphasize the importance of privacy in relation to executive action and decision-making. Recall the case discussed in the previous chapter: the UK government's refusal to disclose the British Cabinet minutes from March 2003, in which military action in Iraq was deliberated. When in the Statement of Reasons, the Attorney General argued that disclosure would be detrimental to, among others, the effective operation of Cabinet government, he articulated this argument in terms of the executive need for privacy:

> Conventions on Cabinet confidentiality are of the greatest pertinence when the issues at hand are of the greatest sensitivity. . . . Ministers must have the confidence to challenge each other *in private*. Decisions of this nature will not however take place without a *private* space in which thoughts can be voiced without fear of . . . publicity. Cabinet provides this space. Disclosure of Cabinet minutes . . . has the potential to . . . compromise the integrity of this thinking space where it is most needed.[35]

On Westin's view, privacy extends not only to the process of policy formulation but also to implementation. He points out that in certain policy areas, in particular diplomatic, military, and economic, disclosure of governmental policies might undercut them. For example, disclosing defense information might serve the purposes of potential enemies and thus undercut defense policies. By classifying military information records, governments exercise "executive privacy,"[36] which is functionally necessary to protect governmental capacity for action.

I have interpreted Murray's claim that states have a right to privacy along the lines of Westin's argument that presents state privacy as a species of group privacy. States, along with other groups, have a right to privacy by virtue of their capacity for autonomous action *viz.* their capacity to formulate and act on their organizational goals (unless they engage in immoral actions).

Next, I refute Westin's and Murray's arguments. While I acknowledge that their concerns about the quality of decision-making and the implementation of certain policies may impose restraints on the openness of democratic governance, I reject articulating these restraints in terms of a state's right to privacy.

4.4 State privacy and democratic accountability

Recall that in representative democracies the relationship between citizens and state institutions is modeled on the principal-agent relation, in which citizens (principals) authorize the government and legislature (agents) to represent their interests and to act on their behalf and the latter provide an account of their actions with respect to those interests.[37] The application of the model embodies the assumption that the democratic authority of state institutions ultimately derives from those it governs and that it is constrained by their will and interests.

The idea that state institutions are the agents representing the citizens-principals is crucial when reflecting on the state's right to privacy. Given that representatives are put in a position of responsibility in relation to the interests of the governed, they owe an account of how they look after citizens' interests. "In political responsibility," Thomas Christiano writes, "the citizen is the principal and the legislator is the agent. The citizens have primacy; they are the ones to whom the legislators are responsible."[38] Political representation and, more generally, principal-agent relationships then involve accountability understood as a mechanism through which the principals-citizens can voice their policy concerns and have the agents-representatives respond to these concerns. Exactly which aspect of the performance of state institutions is subject to citizens' assessment differs as we move between the delegate model of representation and the trustee model of representation, yet the possibility of assessment and accountability is conceptually inherent in democratic representation.

Whereas neither Westin nor Murray addresses the issue of political accountability, presumably neither of them would like to deny its importance for democratic governance. My contention is, however, that by spelling out the state's claim to restrict access in terms of a state's right to privacy, they conceptually preclude the relationship of accountability between the state and citizens. In other words, the idea of a state's right to privacy is inconsistent with democratic accountability. Recall that privacy, in setting normative boundaries to access to information about the individual and group agents and attention drawn to their actions and engagements, designates material that is nobody's business except that of the agents themselves. Privacy, as Judith DeCew has phrased it, "is a property of types of information and activity viewed . . . as beyond the legitimate concern of others."[39] This means that with regard to private information and activity, the privacy right-holder is not open to evaluation and criticism nor can she be held accountable to society. Privacy so understood correlates with a duty on the part of all others to refrain from seeking the information that the group withholds from them and from interfering with its decisions. From this perspective, to claim that the state has a right to privacy is to claim that there are types of information relating to state institutions, decisions, and processes that are beyond the legitimate concern of citizens, for which the state is not accountable to citizens and concerning which citizens have a duty to refrain from inquiring into. This, in turn, is to deny that citizens can verify whether exercises of power are informed by their will and interests and, for that matter, whether any constraints on the state's action are in place.

This denial of accountability built into the concept of privacy rights is in tension with the requirement of accountability built into the idea of democratic representation. In other words, even if it makes sense to speak of state institutions exercising organizational autonomy in taking decisions and formulating policies on behalf of the citizens, this does not suffice for an ascription to them of a right to privacy. State institutions cannot have a right to privacy against those to whom they are accountable. Government is not a law unto itself on the model of an individual acting within the realm of her privacy. Government officials have to give account of and answer for their actions in settings not of their own choosing and their conduct will be assessed by someone other than themselves. The point can be generalized to other principal-agent relationships. Imagine that I delegate the management of my financial assets to a stockbroker. To the extent that the stockbroker, in managing my money, is acting on her own reason (draws on her expertise to formulate a financial strategy and acts on it), she acts autonomously. But her capacity for autonomous action in managing my money does not suffice to grant her privacy with regard to these actions: it would be absurd to say that what she does with my financial assets is her private business. If her financial investments ruin me, she cannot get away with this just by saying that what she did with my money was her private business for which no explanation is due.

I conclude that groups (just as stockbrokers and other individuals) cannot have a right to privacy against those to whom they are accountable and, thus, democratic states have no right to privacy against their citizens.[40] All this is not to say that Westin's and Murray's concerns about the quality of decision-making and the implementation of certain policies may not impose restraints on the openness of democratic governance. However, articulating these restraints in terms of a state's right to privacy is implausible.

4.5 Privacy and secrecy

Murray's defense of the state's right to restrict access is a gestalt switch in mainstream discussion of this topic, which usually proceeds in terms of secrecy. Murray, following Westin, drops this mainstream conceptual framework and conceives of the state's claim to restrict access in terms of a state's right to privacy instead. Fitting this argument into the framework of democratic theory encounters insurmountable problems. Before closing this chapter, I briefly motivate returning to the traditional way of framing the discussion and explain that secrecy, unlike privacy, can be conceived as a right the performance of which can be seen as a matter of accountability.

Consider first the sense in which secrecy – intentional withholding of information – can be conceived as a right. There are scholars who deny this: they recognize that there is a "right to privacy," but they deny that there is an equivalent "right to secrecy" because an appeal to secrecy has no normative component. For example, Stanley Benn and Gerald Gaus argue that:

> The prescriptive function [of privacy] is tightly tied . . . to the normative use: 'Smith's letter is private (so don't read it)' . . . prescribes a consequent forbearance. . . . Describing the letter as 'secret' . . . points to a *de facto* restriction of access.[41]

If Benn and Gaus are right and secrecy has no normative component, then it would be difficult to see how a normative defense of the state's claim to secrecy could get off the ground. Yet, their denial of a normative character of claims to secrecy is too quick. While it is correct that, in Smith's case, neither his intention to keep the letter secret nor his *de facto* hiding of it has the force to obligate us to refrain from reading it in the way in which Smith's appeal to his privacy would have, the prescriptive component of secrecy may be located elsewhere. What Benn and Gaus overlook, I submit, is that secrecy can be seen as a special right arising out of a relation or transaction between agents. In terms of their example, what if I consent to Smith's keeping the letter secret from me? Imagine that the letter concerns arrangements for my birthday party and that I, excited about the prospect of a surprise, have asked Smith to keep them concealed. In that case, Smith has acquired a right to keep the letter secret from me and I have acquired a duty to refrain from reading it. In this case, an appeal to secrecy can be seen as a right with a prescriptive component.

Note that the prescriptive component of the right to secrecy differs from the prescriptive component inherent in a right to privacy. A right to privacy is a right that belongs to the agent by virtue of her intrinsic properties *viz.* capacity for autonomy. The agent has it, not on account of any special transaction or relationship in which she has been involved but simply on account of what she is – an agent with a capacity for autonomous action. As with other natural or universal rights, a right to privacy exists prior to relations and constrains them. It is this constraint that prevents me from reading Smith's private letter. To the extent that secrecy is a right capable of imposing duties of noninterference on other people, however, it is not in virtue of any intrinsic property of the secret-holder, but in virtue of her relation to those from whom she withholds material, such as the fact that others consent to her concealing material or at least waive their liberty rights to seek and expose the material she conceals. In this sense, a secrecy right is like special rights arising out of contracts and promises, which are created by agents' voluntary actions and would not exist but for these actions. This is the sense, I submit, in which a state's claim to restrict access can be understood in terms of a right to secrecy.

Being a special right, a right to keep information secret is conferred for a reason and it loses its normative grounds if the right-holder exercises it in a way that does not serve it. Verifying whether the right-holder exercises the right in a way that accords with the reason for which the right has been conferred is a matter of accountability. Accountability is understood as a mechanism through which those who have conferred this right upon the agent can voice their concerns and have the right-holder respond to these concerns. In this sense, accountability of the right-holder is a necessary, though not sufficient, condition of the validity of special rights. To the extent that the state has a right to secrecy, it is then accountable for how it exercises this. This raises difficult questions of institutional design (how can citizens hold government to account for secret decisions and processes if their content is withheld from them?) to be addressed in Chapters 5 and 6, but it does not exclude accountability as a matter of principle in the way the state's right to privacy does. Hence, whereas demands for oversight and control have less force with regard to information that is private, they can be legitimately raised with regard to information that is secret.

4.6 Conclusion

In classifying material, states claim a right to restrict access and a correlated obligation on the part of citizens to keep off the classified material. Justifications usually appeal to the necessity of restricting access to information and the positive consequences such restrictions have on advancing the basic interests of the state. In this chapter, I have considered a recent non-consequentialist defense of the state's claim to restrict access that appeals to liberal-democratic rights *viz.* Murray's suggestion to understand the state's claim to restrict access as a right to privacy on the part of states. The argument resembles the claims made by proponents of the necessity argument insofar as privacy rights restricting access to government information are seen as a "functional necessity." Despite the apparent similarity, however, the necessity argument and the argument from privacy locate their normative force in different considerations: according to the necessity argument, what is at stake in government's restriction on access is the way it advances its interests; in Westin's and Murray's framing, what is at stake is the rights that the state holds in virtue of its capacity for agency and autonomous action.

I rejected the privacy-based defense of the state's claim to restrict access on account of its tension with democratic accountability. My argument to this effect turns on the nature of privacy claims, which traditionally designate the sphere of noninterference policed by the agent herself and beyond the legitimate concern of others. Because privacy is a right to not be held accountable, resting a democratic defense of the state's claim to restrict access to information on its right to privacy is an oxymoron. From this perspective, to claim that the state has a right to privacy with regard to, for example, classified programs would commit us to saying that there are types of information relating to state institutions and state activities that are beyond the legitimate concern of citizens and for which the state is not accountable to citizens. To grant this would be to preclude the relationship of accountability between the state and citizens that is at the heart of democratic governance and preclude effective constraints on the state's action.

In the next chapter, I argue that we can understand the practices of classification on the part of states as an exercise of a special right to secrecy. My contention is that secrecy is a special right that is entailed in the authority that democratic states exercise.

Notes

1 This chapter draws from Mokrosinska 2020.
2 Strictly speaking privacy, unlike secrecy, may but need not involve concealment. As Bok puts it, "Privacy need not hide. A private garden need not be a secret garden; a private life is rarely a secret life" (1984, 11). Privacy, as the argument from the state's right to privacy conceptualizes it, refers to concealed material.
3 Westin 1967, 49.
4 Westin 1967, ch. 2; Bloustein 1977.
5 Murray 2011.
6 Murray 2005, 200.
7 Westin 1967, 43.
8 Murray 2011, 512.
9 (Inter)national jurisdiction, for example, the EU General Data Protection Regulation (GDPR) is centered on identifiable individuals, where individuals are defined as "natural persons" (Com (2012) 10 final 2012/0010). Bloustein (1977) argues that while a right to group privacy does not enjoy legal protection, American jurisprudence recognizes it implicitly, for example, business organizations enjoy legal protection of privacy under the rubric of intellectual property and trade secrets; group privacy attaches to professional associations such as when the law protects the privacy of communication between physician and patient or between lawyer and client.
10 DeCew 1997, 60.
11 Westin 1967, 7.
12 Westin 1967, 42.
13 Westin 1967, 7; Murray 2005, 198.
14 Harel 2005, 194–195.
15 Westin 1967, 7.
16 Westin 1967, 43.
17 Westin 1967, 46, 43.
18 For an overview of the current state of discussion, see Ritchie 2015; Floridi 2017.
19 Floridi 2017, 89.
20 Loi and Christen 2020, 210.
21 Narveson 1991.
22 Floridi (2017) argues that even groups without such properties but which share some features in common (e.g., smokers, owners of such and such cars, shoppers of such and such kinds of goods, or sets of persons generated algorithmically and clustered by profiling) qualify as groups that can bear (privacy) rights. For discussion, see Loi and Christen 2020.
23 Sumner 1987, 209.
24 Pettit and Schweikard 2006, 34.
25 See Pettit and Schweikard's (2006) discussion on "discursive dilemmas."
26 Pettit and Schweikard 2006, 34.
27 Westin 1967, 42.
28 Floridi 2017, 85.
29 Floridi 2017, 91.
30 Davis 2006, 120.
31 Dumsday 2008, 176–177.
32 Westin 1967, 49.
33 Bloustein 1977, 257.
34 Westin 1967, 49.
35 Grieve 2012, 3–4, emphasis added.
36 Westin 1967, 43.

37 Pitkin 1967; Christiano 1996.
38 Christiano 1996, 208.
39 DeCew 1997, 60.
40 Note the implications of my argument: states cannot have privacy against citizens to whom they are accountable, but possibly they may have privacy against other states, given that they are not accountable to them. Positing the rights to state privacy in inter-state relations is, however, subject to other challenges. Relations between states are importantly different from relations between a democratic state and its citizens. Not only do they lack a democratic character; some would argue that they resemble a state of nature (e.g., Rolf 2014). From this perspective, positing privacy rights or, for that matter, any rights as governing inter-state relations is questionable. In order to do justice to the complex topic of state privacy in the context of inter-state relations would take me into a domain of international relations far beyond the scope of the present chapter.
41 Benn and Gaus 1983, 12.

5 Democratic authority of government secrecy

5.1 Introduction

Having established, in Chapter 2, that the commitment to transparency does not exclude a degree of secrecy in democratic governance, I set out to explore whether a resort to secrecy can be a legitimate exercise of democratic authority. Chapters 3 and 4 considered arguments according to which government restrictions on access to information are legitimate insofar as they are "functionally necessary" – a claim spelled out in terms of, respectively, considerations of necessity and state privacy. I argued that neither appeals to necessity nor privacy could confer upon secret policies and closed-door decision-making processes the status of legitimate exercises of democratic authority without undermining features inherent in the concept of democratic authority.

In this chapter, I develop an alternative defense of government secrecy. Drawing on the formal features of the traditional concept of political authority, I argue that the political authority democratic states exercise actually involves a right to resort to secrecy. This shifts the normative grounds for secrecy from reasons that government actors might entertain when resorting to secrecy to the nature of the power they hold. Focusing on executive secrecy, I argue that this defense of state secrecy does what the necessity- and privacy-based arguments set out to do but failed: it extends political authority to decisions, programs, and processes that the executive deems functionally necessary to classify. Yet it does this not in virtue of their "functional necessity," but in virtue of the right to rule that democratic states hold. Unlike the necessity- and privacy-based arguments, this defense of state secrecy comes with in-built limits to and a demand that the state account for its resort to secrecy.

I start, in Section 5.2, with a challenge addressed to any project attempting to establish democratic authority of state secrecy. According to the challenge, public knowledge of state policies and processes is an epistemic condition of their legitimacy. On account of the knowledge deficit they generate, secret policies and closed-door decision-making processes fail to satisfy this condition and, thus, cannot be seen as legitimate exercises of democratic authority.

DOI: 10.4324/9781003083733-5

In Section 5.3, I argue that the challenge is misplaced. Drawing on the traditional concept of political authority *viz.* its content-independent character, I argue that the authority of state action is divorced from citizens' knowledge of its content. Section 5.4 draws out the implications of this argument for secret uses of power and claims that the knowledge deficit secret policies and processes generate does not affect their legitimacy; the right to rule held by democratic governments involves a right to rule by classified policies and closed-door processes. The argument is qualified: a state recourse to secrecy, as other exercises of content-independent power, is valid only if it remains within substantive and procedural limitations and there are accountability mechanisms to verify it. Sections 5.5 and 5.6 consider how the substantive and procedural constraints on the exercise of content-independent authority limit the scope of legitimate secrecy. Section 5.7 discusses it from the perspective of the accountability requirement. Holding the state to account for secret uses of power creates difficult questions of institutional design: how can citizens verify whether state secrecy remains within the relevant scope limitation if the knowledge of classified policies and processes is withheld from them? Drawing on research in public administration and intelligence studies, I claim that there can be accountability without direct scrutiny by citizens. Section 5.8 qualifies the scope of my argument. Section 5.9 concludes.

5.2 The challenge

In his seminal work on the role of secrecy in democratic states, Dennis Thompson argues that secret policies and closed-door decision-making processes generate a knowledge deficit that undermines their democratic authority. In a democracy, exercises of political power should be authorized by citizens. Secret uses of power fail on this count because people cannot authorize what they are denied knowledge about. Thompson argues:

> [T]he policies and processes of government must be public in order to secure the consent of the governed. . . . [T]he less that citizens know about a policy . . . the less meaningful is the consent citizens can give to it, the less justifiable is the use of state power to enforce it.[1]

Reasoning along similar lines, Christopher Kutz claims that secrecy "strike[s] at the foundation of government's right to rule."[2] If I am denied knowledge of the state's actions, "I cannot . . . understand myself either as in harmony or in dissonance with my polity," he argues.[3] As such, I cannot consent to or dissent from the state's actions, nor can I articulate my will that is needed to authorize its rule.

By this argument, conferring authority on secret uses of power would require disclosing state secrets so that citizens could form an informed judgment about them. This strategy, however, would eliminate the possibility of secrecy that they would be willing to authorize. It is not possible for citizens to decide that a particular program should be kept secret after they have learned about it and formed an opinion that it should be kept secret after all. Re-classifying the information they have de-classified would be like unscrambling scrambled eggs.

To make progress, one would have to find a way to make an informed judgment on a secret policy without disclosing it. One option, explored by Thompson, would be to judge classified policies and closed-door processes by the general policy aims they are meant to realize. This strategy, he emphasizes, only requires that officials impart "second-order publicity about first-order secrecy"[4] *viz.* admit that the government classifies information in certain policy areas, for what reasons, and pursuant to what processes yet without disclosing the details of classified programs.

Thompson's argument goes some way toward resolving the challenge that state secrecy poses to democratic legitimacy but, as he concedes, not the whole way.[5] Second-order publicity about first-order secrecy enables reviewing the general policy aims classified programs are designed to serve but a judgment of general policy aims fails to engage with the elements of their particular application. Correspondingly, consent expressed at this general level may suffice to authorize the general policy, but it will be insufficiently informed to authorize its particular application. An example in point is public support for the general anti-terrorist policies of the US government after 9/11 and the repugnance with which the NSA surveillance program PRISM was met when it was disclosed in a series of leaks by the former NSA contractor Edward Snowden. Indeed, once it was revealed that American citizens were ensnared in the PRISM surveillance practices, many Americans came to judge the general anti-terrorist policies of the US government differently. It is not unthinkable that they might have opposed the US government decision to enhance anti-terrorist measures if they had known that the particular embodiment of such measures would lead to interception of their internet and communications data. Given the disparity in public assessment of the general anti-terrorist policies of the US government and their particular embodiment in the NSA surveillance program PRISM, it would be implausible to say that the knowledge of the general aim of anti-terrorist policies was sufficient to authorize it.

Remarkably, doubts about assessing classified programs through the general policy aims they are meant to realize were voiced by executive actors following the UK government's refusal to grant a FOIA request to disclose the UK Attorney General's advice to the government confirming the legality of a "precision strike" by which a British citizen, Reyaad Khan, suspected of planning terrorist attacks, had been killed by an RAF drone in Raqqa, Syria.[6] The UK Upper Tribunal for Administrative Appeals (UT) dismissed the government's refusal claiming that even though the details of the strike should remain classified, the general policy principles underpinning the advice could be disclosed by way of meeting the demand for the public's assessment of the legality of the precision strike. For the sake of public assessment, the policy decision should therefore be "rewritten or expressed . . . in a way that did not reveal any of the evidence base that was supplied and considered" focusing instead on the general policy principle underpinning it *viz.* the UK's "inherent right to self-defense" allowing targeted drone strikes against identified individuals who are planning terrorist attacks in the UK.[7] In response to the UT ruling, the government called into question the possibility of scrutinizing the legitimacy of the specific decision at the level of general policy aims:

> [W]hile high-level answers have been given to the Committee's questions, . . . the answers should not be taken as representing the Government's detailed and developed thinking on these complex issues. The need to take any future action would be considered according to the circumstances of each operation.[8]

Both the PRISM and the precision strike cases illustrate, as Thompson conceded, that "[t]here is no substitute for considerations of particulars"[9] in judging executive secrecy.

If the prospects of formulating an informed judgment of classified programs in terms of the general policy aims they are meant to realize are poor, what about judging classified executive programs by considering hypothetical cases? Based on hypothetical cases, citizens or their representatives could identify the circumstances and factors that have to be in place to render the policy legitimate. This strategy is not feasible because in political practice there are infinite (combinations of) contingencies to which classifying government information may be a response. Given that it is unlikely that all the contingencies will be thought of, a judgment of secret policy based on hypothetical cases will not be sufficiently complete to warrant authorization of state action in practice.

If, as Thompson and Kutz assume, public knowledge of state policies and processes is a condition of their authority, the conclusion that executive secrecy lacks democratic authority seems difficult to avoid. Next, I argue that the link between citizens' knowledge of state action and their authorization of state action is less tight than their objection presupposes. Drawing on the traditional concept of political authority, I argue that the authority of state policies, including secret policies, is divorced from citizens' knowledge of their content. From this perspective, the knowledge deficit with respect to secret policies does not affect their authority. The challenge, as formulated by Thompson and Kutz, is misplaced.

5.3 Political authority

Political authority is traditionally defined as possession of a right to rule in a content-independent way.[10] To define political authority as content-independent is to say that the binding force of its directives is detached from their content. This distinguishes authoritative directives from standard cases of reasons for action in which there is a connection between the reason for action and the action to be done, such as when the action is independently desirable, has beneficial consequences, or otherwise has moral merit. Authoritative directives are different in that these factors are not what makes them binding. Their validity "is in the . . . fact that someone in authority has said so," as Joseph Raz puts it,[11] not in what she has said or why she has said it.

The idea that political authority has a content-independent character has a long tradition in modern political philosophy and, as Leslie Green remarks, cannot be abandoned "without abandoning part of any satisfactory analysis of political authority."[12] The idea goes back to Hobbes' *Leviathan*, where Hobbes locates the binding force of authoritative commands in a feature of the source of the command, not a feature of what was commanded. He argues: "Command is where a man saith doe this or doe not do this without expecting other reason than the Will of him who Saith it."[13] This view of authoritative commands has received a powerful re-statement in the works of H.L.A. Hart and Joseph Raz.[14] It was Hart who coined the term "content-independence" to indicate that the binding force of authoritative commands is divorced from their content.

Democratic authority is a species of the genus authority. Most influential theories of democratic authority endorse the idea that democratic states exercise power in a content-independent way.[15] For example, Thomas Christiano says:

> Democratic directives give content independent reasons. . . . Citizens have duties to obey democratic decisions not because of the content of the decision or the consequences of their obedience but because of the source of the decision in the democratic assembly.[16]

Content-independence seems particularly well suited to explain the role of political authority in modern democracies. As many scholars emphasize, under the conditions of disagreement characterizing modern societies, the authority exercised by the state relates to its role in arbitrating disputes and solving coordination problems. In such situations, it is more important that a decision is made rather than what decision is made from the range of options available. The government's role in solving coordination and bargaining problems consists of, among other things, marking certain courses of action as salient. Salient points derive their action-guiding force not from what they prescribe but from the fact that they prescribe it. The content of the prescription, that is, the quality of the action prescribed, is irrelevant to the job it is supposed to do. As David Lewis puts it, a salient point "does not have to be uniquely good; indeed, it could be uniquely bad. It merely has to be unique in some way the subjects will notice, expect each other to notice, and so on."[17]

If government directives serve as a salient guide for action, then it is not their content but the fact that they have been issued that makes them the focus of obligations to obey. If it were the content of directives that made them binding, disagreement about their merits and, consequently, whether citizens have reason to comply with them would upset the mediating and coordinating role of political institutions, which require most citizens to comply with most laws and policies most of the time. Authority bypasses disagreement about the merits of government directives because it abstracts away from the content of particular policies and generates reasons for obedience based on the source of the policies.[18]

Democratic authority derives from those over whom it is exercised. To acknowledge that the political authority democratic states exercise is content-independent is to say the citizens authorize the state's power to take decisions and make policies rather than their content: if policy X is authoritative and binding, it is not because citizens have authorized its specific content but because they have authorized the state's power to make it in the first place. This claim requires a qualification. It might seem that in granting the state a mandate to rule in a content-independent way, citizens grant to it an absolute discretionary power to create normative requirements with any content it chooses, relinquishing any say they have in governance. This understanding of content-independent authority is misleading.

To begin with, political institutions empowered with a right to rule in a content-independent way have no natural claim to people's compliance. They are artificial human creations that receive their mandate to take decisions and make policies from those they govern. This mandate they receive for a reason; that reason grounds their authority but also limits it. The limitations it imposes on the exercise of content-independent authority are substantive and procedural.[19] Roughly, they relate to (1) the reasons for having political authority with a mandate to rule in a content-independent way in the first place and (2) the fact that its directives must have certain institutional features that make it possible for them to be effective.

In this general form, these constraints can be found in the early formulation of content-independent authority in Hobbes. While Hobbes' definition of authority as the will of a commander is often taken to imply that the content-independent authority the commander exercises is constrained by nothing except the commander's own interest and, thus, is unlimited, David Dyzenhaus persuasively argues that this interpretation is unwarranted. He reminds us that Hobbes defines the authority of the sovereign not merely as "a Command of any man to any man; but only of him, whose Command is addressed to one formerly obliged to obey him."[20] Thus, even if it is the will of the sovereign rather than the content of his command that functions as a reason for the action, the sovereign's will is the will addressed to those formerly obliged to obey it. This implies that authoritative directives are valid only if subjects can recognize them as reasons for obedience, which are reasons for having political authority in the first place. Commands that systematically fail to track these reasons are invalid. Thus, for Hobbes, who identifies peace and protection as the end of the commonwealth, the sovereign directive that would command its subjects to seek conflict rather than peace would be invalid. It remains the case, Dyzenhaus emphasizes, that Hobbes formulates these substantive constraints on the content-independent authority in a generic way. His project is to provide an account of political authority whatever the nature of the political regime – monarchy, democracy, or aristocracy.[21] In this sense, his constraints on political authority are minimal and not tailored to foundational values and principles specific regimes aspire to realize. Importantly, they fall short of a complete theory of liberal-democratic order.

For contemporary authors discussing the nature of the authority held by liberal-democratic states, the state's right to rule in a content-independent way is anchored in the principles and values at the foundation of liberal-democratic order. Equality and justice, people's right to political participation, or liberal rights such as free speech or privacy are among the aims liberal-democratic states are meant to secure. These reasons serve also as limits to the content-independent authority of the state: policies and processes that contradict the substantive basis of the authority to rule in a content-independent way are invalid.[22] Verifying whether policies and processes remain within the relevant scope limitations is a matter of accountability. Making it possible for people to determine whether they have the authority they claim to have, accountability is then a necessary (but not sufficient) condition of democratic authority.

Besides substantive constraints on the exercise of content-independent authority, there are also procedural ones. They relate to the form that the authoritative directives must take if they are to be successful in coordinating human behavior toward the aims for which the authority has been instituted. First, to be effective, they must be clear, prospective, stable, and non-contradictory. Directives that are obscure, imprecise, retroactive, or so indeterminate as to have no content cannot guide behavior. In a similar way, directives that are kept hidden from those whose behavior they are meant to regulate fail in their action-guiding power. Second, they must bear formal marks of authority that distinguish them from arbitrary uses of power and unmediated coercion. As Dyzenhaus observes, these procedural criteria on the exercise of content-independent authority – formulated in Hobbes as the requirements of the laws of nature – constitute the minimum content of the rule of law.[23]

I have described the political authority exercised by a democratic state as a right to rule in a content-independent way. For citizens to authorize content-independent power is to authorize the power to take decisions and make policies rather than their content. I said that authoritative decisions and policies are valid only if they remain within the substantive and procedural limitations and there are accountability mechanisms to verify them. These constraints affect, but do not determine, the content of any authoritative decision.[24] Next, I argue that state authority so described extends to secret exercises of power.

5.4 Authority of secrecy

To exercise the right to rule in a content-independent way means to have one's instructions binding irrespective of their content. One way in which scholars put this point is by saying that laws and policies are authoritative even if citizens disagree with them and consider them mistaken. Philip Soper put it thus:

> [A]uthoritative . . . directive . . . requires action even if the authority is mistaken in its evaluation of the action. . . . If authorities expect to be obeyed even if their estimates about what is being done are mistaken, individual deliberation about the content of directives is necessarily irrelevant.[25]

To think otherwise would be to concede that citizens should decide whether or not to be guided by laws or policies by considering their merits case by case. If the authority of laws and policies depended on citizens' judgment of their merits, political authority exercised by the state would make no normative difference to the practical reasoning of its subjects. This would contradict its very nature and purpose.

Consider the implications of this understanding of political authority for the claim that citizens' knowledge of government policies is an epistemic condition of their authority. The idea supporting this claim is that citizens' informed judgment of the content of state policies is required for the purpose of their authorization. Had this idea been correct, then indeed citizens' knowledge of the content of state policies would have been a condition of their authority because it would have been necessary to form the judgment needed to authorize them. Yet given that the authority of state's policies is to be sought outside the citizens' evaluation of their content, citizens' knowledge of the content of state policies is not a factor upon which their authority is predicated.

Detaching the authority of state policies from the citizens' knowledge of state policies creates the conceptual space for extending political authority to secret uses of power. If citizens' evaluation and, thus, knowledge of the details of state policies is not a condition of their authority, then policies, the content of which is unknown to citizens, can be authoritative. This being the case, policies, the content of which people do not know because the state restricts access to it, can also be authoritative. The restriction of access to the content of policies does not undermine their authoritative character because state policies derive their authority neither from their content nor from citizens' judgment of their content. I submit that the right to rule in a content-independent way held by democratic governments involves a right to rule by secret decisions and policies. They can be seen as a special case of policies that have a content-independent authority.

When I claim that secret uses of power can be authoritative, I do not imply that all politics may take place in secret – without citizens' knowing – as long as, for example, a written constitution vesting political authority in the state actors is public. Like any exercise of content-independent authority, secret policies and processes can count as legitimate exercises of authority only if they remain within the (1) substantive and (2) procedural limitations and there are (3) accountability mechanisms to verify it. Next, I consider the implications of the first condition for the legitimate scope of executive secrecy and ask when secrecy can serve the aims for the sake of which political authority has been granted. In the remaining sections, I discuss the implications of the second and third conditions for the scope of legitimate secrecy.

5.5 Scope of legitimate secrecy and the goals of authority

Cases in which secrecy serves the aims for the sake of which political authority has been granted are those in which the benefits of transparency in pursuing these aims run out. These are situations in which, as proponents of the necessity- and privacy-based arguments put it, secrecy is "functionally necessary," for example, situations in which national security, effectiveness of government action, and decision-making would have been compromised by transparency.

By conceding that secrecy that the government deems "functionally necessary" can be authoritative, the argument deriving the state's right to secrecy from the formal features of political authority does what the necessity- and privacy-based defenses of executive secrecy set out to do but failed. However, it would be a mistake to see this argument as their improved version because it locates the legitimate status of executive secrecy in considerations other than its "functional necessity."

In order to see the difference, imagine that the government's resort to secrecy is driven by considerations of necessity. By the argument developed in this chapter, the resort to secrecy is authoritative, given that it is the executive or, in Raz's words, "someone in authority"[26] that has resorted to secrecy. While the executive resorts to secrecy because it considers it to be functionally necessary, the functional necessity of secrecy is not the source of its authoritative character. The executive's judgment about the necessity of secret policies is an evaluative judgment about those policies. On the argument developed here, however, the authority of government policies is content-independent, which is to say that it is detached from evaluative judgments about them. Thus, even if the driving force of secret policies is necessity, it is not necessity that renders executive secrets authoritative but the fact that the decision to resort to secrecy was taken by a political actor with legitimate powers to do so.

The argument I have put forward has, then, a two-tier structure. It is the right to rule in a content-independent way that makes classified executive programs authoritative, yet in order for it to take normative effect, these programs must serve the aims for which political authority has been instituted viz. they must be functionally necessary for these aims. To say that functional necessity is not the source of the authority of secret exercises of power but that it determines the range of classified decisions and programs that can be authoritative is to say that functional necessity is only a necessary condition of content-independent authority taking effect in this case but not a sufficient one. In a similar way, the value of truth determines the range of promises that are binding, but this does not mean that the promises derive their binding force from the value of truth.

Shifting the normative grounds for secrecy from reasons of necessity that the actors exercising political authority might entertain when resorting to secrecy to the nature of the power they hold has implications for the scope of legitimate secrecy. Unlike the necessity- and privacy-based arguments, which had difficulties in setting limits to the state's power to resort to secrecy, the argument deriving the state's right to secrecy from the formal features of political authority comes with in-built limits to the state recourse to secrecy. In Chapter 3, we saw that the necessity argument inevitably sends the executive power to resort to secrecy down a slippery slope toward unlimited power. The argument developed in this chapter does not legitimate secret uses of power across the board. Content-independent authority is always limited and given that secret policies can be seen as a special case of policies that have a content-independent authority, these limits apply to them too. Thus, even if government resort to secrecy is motivated by considerations of necessity, the appeals to necessity, which typically elude normative codification, are harnessed and constrained by the considerations at the foundation of content-independent authority. The difference between the two arguments bears on the analysis of the examples discussed in the context of the necessity argument. Recall that by the necessity argument, the Polish involvement in the secret CIA extraordinary renditions program was legitimate because it was believed to be necessary to secure basic interests of the state *viz.* national security. According to the argument outlined in this chapter, it lacked legitimacy: as secrecy was used to cover the violation of human rights involved in the "enhanced interrogation techniques" performed on the prisoners kept at black sites, it failed to satisfy the substantive constraints on content-independent power exercised by democratic governments.[27]

Before I proceed, let me signal an alternative form this argument can take using the conceptual resources of the recent wave of scholarship reviving the idea of fiduciary government.

Fiduciary political theory takes its cues from fiduciary law that governs relations in which one person (the fiduciary) is entrusted with discretionary authority for the benefit of another (the beneficiary) such as relations between agents and principals, guardians and wards, attorneys and clients, and corporate officers and the corporation.[28] In law, such relations entail "fiduciary" duties. The standard legal account of fiduciary duty recognizes two bedrock obligations: the duty of loyalty and the duty of care.

According to fiduciary political theory, political authority mirrors the constitutive properties of fiduciary relations in that public officials wield authority for the good of the citizens and in that capacity acquire obligations comparable to those of agents, trustees, and other fiduciaries.[29] As Stephen Galoob and Ethan Leib argue, "[P]ublic officials are fiduciaries solely in virtue of wielding public authority."[30] According to them, the fiduciary approach can be a component of any theory of political authority, democratic, or otherwise: "The fiduciary principle is compatible with extant theories of legitimacy."[31]

In law, fiduciary duties may include duties of confidentiality. For example, a corporate officer ordinarily owes the corporation a duty of confidentiality *viz.* a duty to refrain from sharing the corporation's private business information. One can pursue a similar strategy to argue that when public fiduciaries incur duties of loyalty and care, they also incur derivative duties of secrecy.[32] For example, when policy makers implement rules to safeguard sensitive government information, they may have a basis for so acting in the fiduciary duty of care. Recall that this duty requires them to be diligent, and to exercise their best judgment, in developing policies aimed at advancing the common good. When faced with circumstances where the dangers of sharing information are apparent, particularly in relation to national security, their best judgment may lead them to classify national security information as the most efficient method of promoting the interests of the citizens-beneficiaries. In this way, on the fiduciary theory of political authority, executive secrecy is not merely a matter of a right to rule; it can also be understood in terms of fiduciary duties of care which office holders acquire in virtue of the right to rule they exercise.

I have located the source of the legitimacy of secret policies and processes in formal features of political authority. A resort to secrecy can be an exercise of authority by democratic states because it is inherent in the right to rule with which they are vested, provided they meet the substantive and procedural constraints and there are mechanisms of accountability to verify this. I have argued that the substantive conditions limit the scope of legitimate secrecy to classified policies and processes that are functionally necessary for the aims for which political authority has been instituted. In the following two sections, I consider, first, the effect of the procedural constraints and, second, the effect of the accountability requirement on the scope of legitimate secrecy. One may argue that these conditions do not so much limit the scope of as entirely preclude legitimate secrecy. The procedural constraints upon the exercise of content-independent authority relate to the form authoritative directives must take to be successful in pursuing the aims for which the authority has been instituted. The worry here is that state secrecy makes the exercise of political authority unsuccessful because it undercuts the action-guiding capacity of state decisions and policies and, thereby, their efficacy. Incapable of adhering to procedural constraints, the executive authority's resort to secrecy cannot take normative effect. A similar objection can be raised in terms of the accountability requirement. Secrecy makes it impossible for people to verify whether secret policies and processes remain within the substantive scope limitations and, thus, whether they have the authority they claim to have. Therefore, the accountability requirement does not so much limit the scope of legitimate secrecy as entirely preclude it.

5.6 Scope of legitimate secrecy and the authority's action-guiding power

For content-independent decisions and policies to be valid, they must be effective in coordinating human behavior toward the aims for which the authority has been instituted. This, Raz argues, requires that authoritative directives be capable of being presented as action-guiding directives – that is, as being presented as "someone's (person's or institution's) view as to how citizens should act."[33] Now to present a view as to how citizens should act, one must first communicate it to them and, thus, the capacity to be communicated is a condition that authoritative directives must satisfy. In Raz's words, "what cannot communicate with people cannot have authority over them."[34] Thus, directives and policies that are meant to regulate citizens' actions but, due to their secret character, cannot be communicated to them fail to satisfy the procedural conditions set upon the exercise of political authority. Let me call this the efficacy objection: given that the point of the practical authority exercised by the state is to coordinate social life by issuing directives that guide people's actions, then it is hard to see how coordination can be achieved if the action-guiding directives are secret.

In answering this objection, I draw from a discussion in jurisprudence regarding the validity of secret laws. For both natural law scholars and positivists, publicity is one of the principles of legality in the sense that it is a condition of the law's action-guiding function.[35] At the same time, however, it is acknowledged that not all laws are intended to guide the general public, the implication being that those whose actions the laws are not meant to guide need not know about them. According to Lon Fuller, "[T]he great bulk of modern laws relate to specific forms of activity, such as carrying on particular professions or businesses; it is therefore quite immaterial that they are not known to the average citizen."[36] Hart points out that a law's action-guiding force may be confined to officials, in which case there is no need to make it known to ordinary citizens. In an extreme case, it is only officials whose conduct the law is intended to guide.[37] This creates a conceptual space for secret laws. Insofar as secret laws are meant to guide someone's actions, the fact of concealment does not deprive them of validity. Raz put this point thus:

> I do not mean to suggest that all laws are open. Secret laws are possible provided that they are not altogether secret. Someone must know their content some of the time. They are publicly ascertainable and they guide the

behavior of the officials to whom they are addressed or who are charged with their enforcement by being so.[38]

In the same way in which secrecy need not undermine the validity of laws, it need not void the authority of state policies. This is the case to the extent that secret policies coordinate the actions of only a subsection of all citizens, say only the members of intelligence services, the military, or the police. Foreign intelligence gathering programs are an example in point: they are meant to be action-guiding for intelligence agents but not for citizens. When state directives guide the actions of intelligence agents but not of citizens, the efficacy objection requires transparency only with regard to the addressees of the directives, that is, the intelligence agents. With respect to citizens at large, however, the secrecy of the directives does not undermine their action-guiding power because foreign intelligence programs have no action-guiding power for citizens in the first place. With regard to citizens, then, the efficacy objection does not prohibit the secrecy of foreign intelligence programs.

Consider also state actions that are not action-guiding at all, for example, political negotiations conducted behind closed doors. Negotiations are ways of arriving at action-guiding directives and policies, but they are not action-guiding themselves. As they are not action-guiding, it is not the case that secrecy endangers their action-guiding power. As there is no action-guiding power that secrecy endangers here, the efficacy objection does not prohibit the secrecy of closed-door political negotiations. I conclude that the objection leaves an important class of secret uses of power intact.

5.7 Scope of legitimate secrecy and the accountability of office holders

The idea that democratic authority derives from those it governs implies that it is constrained by their will and interests. In order to verify whether the actions of those in power are so informed and, thus, whether they possess the claimed authority, the people have a right to control and hold them to account: voice their policy concerns and have them respond to them.

The necessity- and privacy-based defenses of secrecy had difficulty accommodating the accountability principle. Anchoring the legitimacy of secret uses of power in considerations of necessity made the accountability principle subject to suspension whenever necessity would require it; spelling it out in terms of privacy, defined as a right to not be held accountable, excluded it altogether. The argument locating the legitimacy of executive secrecy in the formal features of political authority exercised by democratic states comes with in-built accountability demands: given that the state's right to resort to secrecy is a special case of its right to rule in a content-independent way, those who grant that authority are entitled to verify whether the right-holder – the state – exercises it in accordance with the reason for which it has been granted.

Even though the demands for accountability are a necessary (but not sufficient) condition of the authority to resort to secrecy, their institutional implementation is not straightforward. A concern about secret policies and processes is that they disable the mechanisms of democratic accountability, for how can citizens call their representatives to account and verify whether secret uses of power remain within the relevant substantial and procedural side-constraints if the knowledge of their content is withheld from them? As Kutz puts it, "[S]ecrecy undermines democratic accountability, raising the possibility that we do not know what our government does in our name, and so cannot demand a change."[39] Transparency is imperative, the argument goes, because it is a prerequisite of democratic accountability. "At a minimum," Thompson writes, "democracy requires that citizens be able to hold officials accountable, and to do that citizens must know what officials are doing and why."[40] Only if state policies and decisions are given adequate publication can people ascertain whether policies remain within the relevant scope limitations.

The problem with democratic control over and accountability for secret uses of power has received much attention from public administration and legal scholars.[41] Drawing on the relevant discussions, I argue that transparency is sufficient for accountability but by no means necessary. There exist forms of accountability that do not require disclosure to the general public and direct citizen scrutiny.

Two alternative mechanisms of control and accountability are of special interest. A first mechanism is retrospective disclosure *viz*. public disclosure of previously classified material when it has lost its sensitive character. Most states have institutionalized retrospective disclosure by either setting a time limit to the classification period or conducting periodic review procedures of classified documents.[42] Yet whereas retrospective disclosure of previously classified documents makes it possible for citizens to investigate the secret policy, detect possible wrongdoing, and call its authors to account, it offers little opportunity to take remedial measures.

A second mechanism of control and accountability does not involve disclosure to the general public. It is disclosure only to discrete groups of people, for example, specialized parliamentary or judicial committees acting on behalf of citizens. Oversight committees can be seen as an intermediate layer of democratic accountability mediating between decision-makers and citizens. Forms of accountability in modern democracies are often, as Jeremy Waldron calls them, "layered and mediated,"[43] for example, civil servants are accountable to the cabinet minister, cabinet ministers are accountable to a legislative committee, and the members of parliamentary committees mediate ultimate accountability to the people who elect them. The scope and kind of information disclosed at these different layers vary. Oversight committees, which call the executive to account, have the task of deciding whether the classification policy is within the procedural and substantial scope limitations of democratic authority. In order to perform this task, they are vested with the right to pose questions, issue resolutions, launch inquiries, and conduct study missions. On the basis of this information but without disclosing it publicly, they owe citizens the assurance that the restriction on information has been done for legitimate reasons. Oversight committees can ensure a timely response to secret uses of power and in this sense have an advantage over the retrospective disclosure mechanism.

Pointing to oversight committees as an alternative to the disclosure of government information to the general public is not to deny that they face important challenges. For one, as Rahul Sagar points out, given that the committees must do their work in camera, the problem emerges of "who guards the guardians?"[44] When the oversight committee's work is shielded from public view, the overseers might turn a blind eye to controversial uses of secret power. This danger is particularly acute when a majority of the committee members are affiliated with the governing party. Marina Caparini argues:

> In the parliamentary system the executive . . . is drawn from the legislature. . . . Since the executive is accountable to the legislature, party discipline is strictly maintained. Political deference may have significant influence on the functioning of parliamentary committees, where members of the majority or coalition governing party are unwilling to criticize a Minister and the domain under his management.[45]

For another, oversight committees depend on the willingness of the secret holders to provide classified information. If the secret holders themselves will not provide it, or provide only those pieces of classified information that support their preferred policy choices, then the committee's work is thwarted because there will be little information available that is independent and useful.

Arguably, these shortcomings have been among factors why such oversight bodies have performed poorly over the past decades adopting, as Richard Aldrich and Daniela Richterova observed, a deferential approach vis-à-vis the executive branch.[46] While a full response to these challenges deserves a separate study in institutional design of oversight mechanisms, some insights can be gained from the studies of oversight of intelligence services.[47] They point to adjustments in the institutional design of oversight committees, their stature, and the way they interact with the secret keepers as factors that may contribute to overcoming the problems indicated previously.

In order to maintain oversight objectivity and avoid overseers becoming too closely identified with the executive, it is considered desirable to strive for an adversarial composition of the membership of oversight committees *viz.* including members of opposition parties so that they, as well as the parties in power, may challenge governments. Kim Scheppele draws on the example of the German system of oversight, which is chaired by the majority and minority parties on a rotating basis and operates under the premise that "the opposition parties must be able to check that majority parties are not using the intelligence services for their own political purposes."[48] True, even an adversarial composition could pursue its own partisan agenda. In such cases, however, the task may be delegated to a panel of independent experts acting on reasons rather than interests.

Another way to discipline the overseers is to introduce multiple stages of oversight. Heidi Kitrosser proposes that information might first be channeled to a small group, which has the power (through majority vote or other mechanism) to determine that the information or parts thereof should be transmitted to a different group.[49] The possibility that the proceedings of the committee become in this way more widely available creates some incentive for the committee to act responsibly.

With regard to the problem of the dependency of oversight committees on the political will of those they are to oversee, the challenge is to overcome the secret-holders' reluctance to comply with reporting requirements. Kitrosser argues that the resistance of the executive to providing information to the oversight bodies relates to the fear that it will be leaked:

> Whether reasonable or not, fears may arise that the more persons notified – even within the relatively secure realm of the intelligence committees – the greater the likelihood of leakage. More cynically, such fears may provide an easy and politically palatable excuse for avoiding . . . disclosures.[50]

Among the measures to deal with this problem, Kitrosser recommends adjustment of the oversight committees' structure and size via reassessment of security clearance requirements. The group of overseers must be sufficiently large in terms of their capacities and powers to understand the information conveyed and to have a real chance of influencing the programs of which they are informed but small enough to minimize the chances of leaks.[51] Further measures meant to induce the executive's compliance with reporting requirements include installing repetitive interactions between the executive and the overseers and increasing the committees' general powers, stature, competence, and influence (even the authority to wield a power to subpoena of their own): "[H]eightening committees' prestige, visibility and abilities, such changes could increase the political incentives for committees to demand information and for the executive branch to comply with such demands."[52]

Finally, Aldrich and Richterova have postulated strengthening accountability mechanisms that go beyond national oversight structures and rely on collaboration and information sharing between different oversight bodies, national and international, formal and informal. Insofar as such "ambient accountability" mechanisms[53] comprising external bodies are able to collaborate on investigations and are more immune to executive pressure from national governments than national oversight bodies, their intervention could prove important in providing effective democratic control and accountability of state secrecy.

To the extent that these institutional arrangements ameliorate the credibility of oversight committees, state secrecy need not be an obstacle to control and accountability.

5.8 Scope of legitimate secrecy: shallow, Glomar, and deep secrets

I have argued that democratic states have a right to resort to secrecy in virtue of the right to rule in the content-independent way with which they are vested. My argument does not defend state secrecy across the board: I have indicated that the authoritative status of secret uses of power takes normative effect only when they are functionally necessary, satisfy the substantive and procedural side-constraints, and there are mechanisms of accountability to verify this. In this section, I qualify my argument further.

Sociologists, political scientists, and legal scholars have distinguished between shallow and deep secrets and applied this distinction to secrets of state.[54] Shallow secrets are those of which citizens know the existence even though they are ignorant of their content. For example, citizens know that intelligence services gather information on terrorist suspects, but they do not know the content of the information-gathering programs. Deep secrets are secrets the existence of which citizens are not aware, for example, if they have no idea that the intelligence services gather suspect-related information of any kind. A third, less discussed, category of secrets includes records for which classification rules exist but governments refuse to confirm the actual presence or absence of classified records implying that confirmation of their (non-)existence would be equivalent to disclosing their very content. For example, in response to a request for information relating to a terrorist suspect, the intelligence agency may respond thus: "We can neither confirm nor deny that our agency has any records matching your request. Hypothetically, if such records were to exist, the subject matter would be classified, and could not be disclosed."[55] I will refer to secrets of this type as "Glomar secrets" using the label such responses have received in US jurisdiction.[56] Later, I argue that the executive authority resorting to secrecy can take normative effect with regard to shallow and, arguably, Glomar secrets but not with regard to deep secrets.

In Section 5.5, following Raz, I argued that insofar as state policies are meant to be action-guiding for citizens, they must be capable of being communicated to them. I denied that this argument refutes the authority of secret policies insofar as the content of such policies is not meant to be action-guiding for citizens (as opposed, e.g., to intelligence agents). Note, however, that insofar as secret policies restrict citizens' access to the details of classified information, the restriction itself is meant to be action-guiding. From this perspective, one may meaningfully ask about the authoritative status of the restriction of access secret policies involve. Shallow, Glomar, and deep secrets register differently on this count.

With regard to shallow secrets, the state keeps certain information secret from citizens but communicates the fact of secrecy by flagging it as "classified." In communicating the restriction on access, the state communicates (1) that the content of the policy is not meant to be action-guiding for them and (2) its will with regard to how citizens should act in relation to classified information *viz.* that they refrain from seeking and disclosing it. For example, if the executive labels the operations of intelligence agencies classified, (1) it communicates that the regulations with regard to collecting intelligence information are not action-guiding for citizens and (2) it imparts its will with regard to how citizens should act in relation to classified intelligence information *viz.* that they refrain from seeking and disclosing it. Correspondingly, citizens are able to identify the restriction as an action-guiding directive. From this perspective, then, the restriction on access involved in shallow secrets is action-guiding and authoritative. The case of deep secrecy is different. In this case, the restriction on access to such programs is itself secret and cannot be communicated to those whose access it is meant to restrict. As this restriction is itself kept secret and, thus, incapable of being communicated to those whose access it is meant to restrict, it is incapable of being action-guiding for them. Failing on this count, the executive authority's resort to secrecy fails to take normative effect. Glomar secrets occupy the middle ground between shallow and deep secrets. They are akin to deep secrets in that it is not only the content of classified information but also the actual decision to classify it that is withheld from citizens. However, unlike in the case of deep secrecy, a Glomar response by the executive, implying that if these records existed they would be classified, provides some notice to the public that the executive may act on secret grounds. Insofar as this response communicates that citizens should refrain from further inquiry, it is action-guiding in the way required of authoritative directives.

The exercise of democratic authority requires that citizens be able to hold officials to account. Arguably, this condition can be satisfied with regard to shallow secrets. Here, even though citizens do not know the contents of the classified program, they know that a classified program is in force and, thus, the demand for accountability can be raised. As long as it can be raised and the mechanisms of accountability discussed in the previous section are in place, their legitimate status is not precluded. When deep secrets are at issue, citizens are kept in the dark about their very existence. If a classified program cannot even be thought of as a possible subject of accountability, accountability is precluded. Failing on this count, deep secrets fall beyond the scope of legitimate exercises of authority. Glomar secrets resemble deep secrets because they involve withholding both the information and the decision to classify it, removing them from oversight through publicly established accountability mechanisms. Unlike deep secrecy, however, the government's denial to confirm the actual presence or absence of classified records acknowledges that the executive may resort to secrecy. Therefore, a Glomar response indicates that further investigation regarding an issue may be warranted and does not hinder citizens or their representatives from questioning those responsible for keeping secrets.[57] At the very least an independent assessment of the risk involved in confirming or denying the actual existence of classified material can be requested. In some jurisdictions, courts request such an assessment in the context of covert operations of law enforcement agencies. For example, in the UK, for each case in which disclosure is requested but the police refuse to confirm or deny the existence of the requested records, the courts require the police to provide an independent assessment of the risk that confirmation or denial of the requested records could involve. Katerina Hadjimatheou, who analyses secrecy in undercover policing in the UK, suggests extending this mechanism to Glomar secrets more broadly. Just as an independent risk assessment is an instrument toward holding the police accountable for Glomar responses so could it provide grounds for holding state officials to account in cases of Glomar secrets. As she puts it:

> [A]ccountability in a democracy does not require disclosure of all information held by the state, nor even of the specific reasons why such information should be protected. . . . But it does require some objective reassurance that such reasons in fact exist, which is precisely what risk assessments are designed to provide.[58]

Subject to such control mechanisms, Glomar secrets would become comparable to shallow secrets and so would their legitimacy status.

I conclude that different kinds of executive secrecy exercise different degrees of democratic legitimacy: while shallow secrets and, arguably, Glomar secrets can be seen as a legitimate exercise of democratic authority, deep secrets fail on this count.

Limiting the range of legitimate secrecy to shallow and, arguably, Glomar secrets marks yet another difference between the defense of secrecy developed in this chapter and the defenses of secrecy that derive their authority directly from their "functional necessity." Recall that by the necessity argument, programs kept in deep secrecy such as the Manhattan program were legitimate. By the argument anchoring the legitimacy of state secrecy in the formal features of political authority, such programs lack legitimacy.

5.9 Conclusion

This chapter argued that secret uses of power by democratic states can be a legitimate exercise of democratic authority. My argument has drawn on the formal features of political authority *viz.* its content-independent character. I argued that as long as we have no problem with authorizing the content-independent power of democratic states, we should also have no problem with authorizing the policies and decisions that democratic states classify as secret. My argument is limited to shallow secrets that are functionally necessary, remain within substantive and procedural limits, and there are accountability mechanisms in place to verify this. The case may be made that this could extend to Glomar secrets, too.

Notes

1 Thompson 1999, 182, 184.
2 Kutz 2009, 199.
3 Kutz 2009, 214.
4 Thompson 1999, 185.
5 Thompson 1987, ch. 1.
6 For a discussion, see Thomas 2020.
7 [2017] UKUT 495 (AAC), 21.
8 Quoted after Thomas 2020, 151.
9 Thompson 1987, 29.
10 The following two sections draw from Mokrosinska 2019.
11 Raz 1986, 35.
12 Green 1988, 239. But see critiques of content-independence by Markwick 2003; Klosko 2011.
13 Hobbes 2003, ch. 25, 176.
14 Hart 1982, ch. 10; Raz 1979, ch. 12.
15 This is clear for procedural accounts of democracy, which condition the authority of democratic procedures on their intrinsic value, see for example Christiano 2008; Lefkowitz 2005; Viehoff 2014. Accounts of democratic authority that combine proceduralist with instrumentalist (epistemic) elements condition the authority of democratic procedures on their ability to produce decisions that track the procedure-independent truth. These accounts also endorse content-independent nature of democratic authority, see Estlund 2007, 118–119. Instrumentalist accounts derive the authority of democracy from the fact that democratic decision-making procedures more reliably produce decisions that are substantively better than those produced by non-democratic procedures (Arneson 2003). These accounts lend themselves to differing interpretations. Valentini (2018) sees them as basing political authority on content-dependent reasons, which, as Adams (2017) argues, has the problematic consequence that authority makes no normative difference to practical reasoning of its subjects. Others claim that instrumentalist accounts adopt the logic of rule consequentialism and establish content-independent authority similarly to the way rule consequentialism does so (Mokrosinska 2012, 187, n. 22).
16 Christiano 2008, 261, 252, 244.
17 Lewis 1969, 35.
18 Raz 1986, ch. 3; Viehoff 2014, 370; Adams 2017, 151–154.
19 Dyzenhaus 2001; Christiano 2008; Adams 2017.
20 Hobbes 2003, ch. 26, 159.
21 Dyzenhaus 2001, 474.
22 Christiano 2008, ch. 7; Adams 2017, 152–154.
23 Dyzenhaus 2001.
24 While side-constraints limit the normative force of content-independent directives, they do not provide them with normative force. It is one thing to show that the political authority does not violate certain fundamental moral principles or values but quite another to have to show that it is justified by them.
25 Soper 1989, 221.
26 Raz 1986, 35.
27 Bodnar and Pudzianowska 2010.

28 Frankel 2011.
29 Criddle et al. 2018. Proponents of this approach have not addressed the problem of secrecy in governance, but the line of argument I suggest is congenial to their approach.
30 Galoob and Leib 2018, 166.
31 Galoob and Leib 2018, 169.
32 Cf. Bruno 2019.
33 Raz 1995, 202.
34 Raz 1995, 201.
35 Hart (1997) speaks of the principle of intelligibility; Fuller (1969) of the principle of promulgation.
36 Fuller 1969, 51.
37 Hart 1997, 117.
38 Raz 1979, 51, n. 9.
39 Kutz 2009, 200.
40 Thompson 1999, 182.
41 Caparini 2007; Kitrosser 2008; Colaresi 2014.
42 For country overview, see Földes 2016.
43 Waldron 2016, 168.
44 Sagar 2007, 413–414.
45 Caparini 2007, 14.
46 Aldrich and Richterova 2018, 1010.
47 Caparini 2007.
48 Scheppele 2006, 619.
49 Kitrosser 2008, 1072.
50 Kitrosser 2008, 1076. For the opposing view, Sagar 2013, 88.
51 Kitrosser 2008, 1071.
52 Kitrosser 2008, 1088.
53 Aldrich and Richterova 2018.
54 Gutmann and Thompson 1996; Pozen 2010.
55 This formulation is modeled on the CIA response to media queries about the existence of a secret CIA project to recover a sunken Russian submarine with nuclear missiles, see Flowers 2015, 345.
56 Phillippi v. CIA, 546 F. 2d 1009, 1011 (D.C. Cir. 1976).
57 Cf. Gosseries and Parr 2021, 1.4.2.
58 Hadjimatheou 2017, 294.

6 Legislative secrecy in deliberation and voting[1]

Co-Authored with Suzanne Bloks

6.1 Introduction

In democratic government, legislative assemblies exercise content-independent political authority. As per the argument developed in the previous chapter, their resort to secrecy can be authoritative provided certain limiting conditions are satisfied. Rather than rehearsing the argument to that effect, this chapter contributes to the reflections on the conditions that make the assembly's authority to resort to secrecy take normative effect. It proposes that this is the case when its resort to secrecy is functionally necessary to preserve the legislative capacity to act.

Democratically elected legislatures are collective decision-making bodies representing citizens. They are, as Mark Warren and Jane Mansbridge put it, the most democratic of all the branches of government in that they come closer than the other branches to representing and communicating with the people in all of their plurality.[2] As the official law-giving bodies, legislatures convert people's wills into a collective decision and empower them to act. The legislature's capacity to act, Warren and Mansbridge claim, is then "a crucial component of democratic governance. . . . When legislatures deadlock . . . their inaction undermines key democratic values."[3]

It is commonly believed that openness should be the norm of parliamentary decision-making: open settings guarantee the best decisions and facilitate compromise, if not consensus,[4] and in this sense, they are a condition for the legislative capacity to act. Legislative decision-making has two main components: deliberation and voting. As far as parliamentary deliberation is concerned, the empirical findings, reviewed in Chapter 2, qualify the conviction about the salutary effects of publicity. Publicity has been shown to introduce populist or plebiscitary[5] dynamics into processes of legislative deliberation, threatening a deadlock. In light of these findings, democratic scholars have acknowledged that there are conditions under which legislative deliberation may take place behind closed doors, provided mechanisms of accountability are in place.

The impact of publicity on legislative voting has received no systematic attention in the discussion of secrecy and transparency in democratic

DOI: 10.4324/9781003083733-6

governance.[6] This chapter contributes to this unexplored theme. Following recent developments in democratic theory which present voting and deliberation as complementary rather than competing models for democratic decision-making,[7] it argues that the same reasons that support moving parliamentary deliberations behind closed doors also support moving parliamentary voting behind closed doors.

The argument unfolds as follows. Section 6.2 reviews reasons for moving legislative deliberation behind closed doors in situations in which it reaches an impasse inhibiting legislative capacity to act. Section 6.3 examines voting deadlocks that inhibit the legislative capacity to act. Section 6.4 argues that resolving voting deadlocks requires that legislators adjust their votes in the course of an additional sequence of deliberation and voting. Section 6.5 argues that the second round of deliberation and voting should be moved behind closed doors. Section 6.6 takes up the question of democratic accountability of legislators for outcomes of deliberation and voting behind closed doors. Section 6.7 concludes.

6.2 Decision-making settings and legislative (in)capacity to act

To make laws and policies, legislators have to resolve their disagreements and negotiate compromises.[8] It has been recognized that the format of deliberative settings – their open- or closed-door character – makes representatives adopt different stances toward the policy issues at hand and, thus, is an important factor determining the outcome of legislative deliberation.[9]

According to early deliberative democrats, open settings have epistemic and political benefits. Regarding their epistemic benefits, open deliberation settings would produce better arguments because they would discipline representatives to scrutinize all relevant facts, consider alternative positions, and carefully articulate their arguments. Regarding their political benefits, open settings would encourage reasoning in terms of impartial considerations and public interest or, at least, deter a politics of self-interest. The force of the better argument and appeals to general interest, early deliberative democrats believed, would pave the way to an agreement.[10]

Empirical research has qualified this belief, demonstrating that publicity may also have the opposite effects. Open settings introduce an audience to the deliberation site. In the presence of cameras, legislators may become concerned about how their arguments will affect their re-election. They may become more concerned to please their audiences and score points against their adversaries rather than cooperate and support the policy proposals they judge best. As Olympia Snowe, a former US senator observed:

> Much of what occurs in Congress today is what is often called 'political messaging.' Rather than putting forward a plausible, realistic solution to a

> problem, members on both sides offer legislation that is designed to make a political statement. Specifically, the bill or amendment is drafted to make the opposing side look bad on an issue and it is not intended to ever actually pass.[11]

As political messaging replaces policy-making, the legislative process turns into a campaigning tool. The more the logic of campaigning intrudes into policy-making, the more the epistemic and political benefits of deliberation fade. For one, plebiscitary campaigning rhetoric lowers the quality of arguments and debate. Legislators skip policy aspects that they consider too complex for the public to appreciate, leave relevant facts unexamined, and do not take all views into consideration. Without a thorough analysis of the policy issue at stake and based on low-quality argument, the compromise, if any, may turn out unworkable and unstable and the policy adopted fragile and likely to misfire. For another, the logic of campaigning induced by publicity inhibits compromise. Reaching a compromise requires what Amy Gutmann and Dennis Thompson call a "compromising mindset"[12]: political actors accept changing their positions and renounce part of the realization of their own principles. The campaigning mindset, however, precludes the compromising mindset: as Gutmann and Thompson argue, it makes legislators see their opponents as adversaries who must be defeated rather than co-legislators who should be worked with.[13] In effect, it makes them unwilling to make concessions and reluctant to change their mind even in light of better arguments. As former US Senator, James B. Pearson put it, "[N]obody wants to admit in public that he was wrong."[14] Publicity strengthens the uncompromising mindset: for fear of being judged unprincipled by their constituents, legislators are reluctant to change or shift positions. As Brian Kogelmann observes, "[F]ew things are worse for a politician than being labeled a flip-flopper. . . . [C]itizens generally dislike it when those representing them change their positions. This incentivizes politicians to remain steadfast, which makes compromise difficult."[15]

As plebiscitary and adversarial rhetoric fuels disagreement and the lack of flexibility decreases chances for finding political common ground, impasse looms large. "The legislators," Warren and Mansbridge argue, "fail to agree and thus fail to act."[16] Legislative deadlocks lead to deficits in democratic decision-making because they disempower people: when citizens press for change, legislative impasse makes it impossible for them to implement it.

When public deliberation threatens to reach a deadlock, closing the doors of the deliberation site promises to break the impasse. Closed-door settings eliminate the audience and thereby the logic of campaigning, which disrupts the process of parliamentary deliberation. Negotiation scholars observe that closed-door settings stimulate serious discussion and produce better arguments; by creating a space in which legislators can try out ideas and change their minds without fear of losing face, they facilitate compromise. Both historical examples and contemporary political practice provide evidence on the epistemic and political benefits of closed-door interactions. Thus, James Madison argued that secrecy of the proceedings of the Constitutional Convention of Philadelphia of 1787 was integral to its success because it allowed delegates to revise their positions over the course of the debate:

> Had the members committed themselves publicly at first, they would have afterwards supposed consistency required them to maintain their ground, whereas by secret discussion no man felt himself obliged to retain his opinions any longer than he was satisfied of their propriety and truth, and was open to the force of argument.[17]

The General Secretariat of the Council of the EU appealed to similar arguments when in 1994 it defended the secrecy of its proceedings in a lawsuit launched by a journalist who contested the Council's decision not to grant him access to some documents:

> The Council normally works through a process of negotiation and compromise, in the course of which its members freely express their national preoccupation and positions. If agreement is to be reached, they will frequently be called upon to move from those positions . . . on a particular point or points. This process, vital to the adoption of Community legislation, would be compromised if delegations were constantly mindful of the fact that the positions they were taking, as recorded in Council minutes, could at any time be made public through the granting of access to these documents, independently of a positive Council decision.[18]

Cornelia Ulbert and Thomas Risse found that closed-door settings during European Council summits enabled political actors to escape negotiation deadlock "because negotiators do not have to stick to their fixed preferences behind closed doors and are allowed to 'think out loud' about possible negotiating solutions."[19]

In light of the empirical evidence for epistemic and political benefits of closed-door deliberation, deliberative democrats, Simone Chambers, Jane Mansbridge, and Mark Warren among others, have come to qualify the unconditional presumption in favor of publicity of political deliberation, conceding that in the face of a deliberative impasse, it is closed-door rather than open settings that are a condition of the legislative capacity to act.[20]

While the impact of publicity on legislative deliberation has been widely discussed, much less attention has been paid to the impact of publicity on legislative voting. Recent work by Kogelmann has opened up this unexplored theme in the discussion of transparency and secrecy in governance.[21] Kogelmann argues that legislators ought not only to deliberate behind closed doors for the reasons indicated previously, they also ought to vote by secret ballot in much the same way in which citizens vote by secret ballot in general elections. Open voting settings make legislation vulnerable to elite capture allowing "the rich and powerful to buy off politicians"[22] in return for their effort to advance the interests of the contributors. They also increase the capacity of organized interest groups to monitor and eventually influence the legislative process in a way that ordinary citizens are not capable of. Secrecy reduces the unequal influence of money and the power of special interest groups on legislation and thereby better serves democratic equality. Kogelmann concludes that secrecy of parliamentary voting is preferred because "[d]emocratic equality . . . thrives in darkness."[23]

This chapter contributes to this emerging track of critical transparency scholarship by offering yet another rationale for secrecy of legislative voting. We argue that just as legislative deliberation in open settings may lead to a deadlock, so can voting. Taking the cue from the discussion of the impact of publicity on deliberation, we submit that closed-door settings (i.e., secret with regard to citizens but open with regard to peer legislators) overcome legislative voting gridlocks just as they overcome deliberation gridlocks. The legislative assembly's authority to resort to secrecy takes normative effect when it is functionally necessary to restore its capacity to act.

6.3 Voting deadlocks in parliamentary decision-making

Like all other collective decision-making bodies, legislatures are vulnerable to decision-making problems when attempting to reach collective goals. Legislators often agree on policy goals – such as reducing unemployment, calming the housing market, or providing security – but disagree on the specific policies by which to achieve those goals. Failing to reach a compromise on how to achieve the policy goals, they fail to solve major issues in society, a failure for which the electorate is likely to hold them accountable. In social choice theory, such collective decision problems go under the name of "doctrinal paradox."[24]

The doctrinal paradox describes a situation in which the majority of representatives (MPs/political parties) intends to reach a policy goal and votes for a number of different legislative proposals to do so, yet few or none of the proposals individually has enough support to be implemented and, hence, parliament ends up with a policy program that does not reach the policy goal. In other words, the doctrinal paradox describes a paradoxical distribution of votes that leads to a legislative deadlock on a policy goal.[25]

In order to introduce the doctrinal paradox, consider a policy goal to reduce greenhouse gas emissions by 49% by 2030, compared to 1990 levels. This is the target of the EU and its Member States.[26] Assume that a majority in parliament intends to reach this policy goal. Assume also, for simplicity's sake, that there are three legislative proposals to reach the goal of greenhouse gas emissions reduction: heftier diesel taxes (greens in favor), building nuclear power plants (liberals in favor), and subsidies for insulating social housing (socialists in favor). A legislative proposal is implemented if it is accepted by a majority in parliament. Further assume that it is not necessary to implement all three legislative proposals in order to reach the goal, that all representatives have reason to reject at least one of the three proposals, and that the representatives know which combination of legislative proposals would be sufficient to achieve the policy goal.

Given the preferences of the representatives on the three legislative proposals, there are two ways to determine whether a parliamentary majority intends to reach the policy goal: a *proposal-driven* way and a *goal-driven* way.[27] In the proposal-driven method, the majority opinion is determined per legislative proposal. Representatives vote on each of the legislative proposals and let the majority view on each proposal determine whether or not it is collectively endorsed. We say that the majority opinion is extracted from representatives' *disaggregate* preferences. Whether the policy goal is reached depends on the number of legislative proposals that gain majority support. By contrast, in the goal-driven method, whether the parliament supports the policy goal depends on the representatives' *aggregate* preferences. In this case, we determine for each representative whether they intend to reach the policy goal on the basis of the number of proposals that they support. This is their aggregate preference for the policy goal. If a majority in parliament expresses an aggregate preference, we conclude that there is parliamentary support for reaching the policy goal. Hence, the core difference between the proposal-driven and goal-driven interpretation is the order in which the majority opinion and the aggregate over the proposals are taken. In the proposal-driven method, the majority opinion is determined *before* the proposals are aggregated; in the goal-driven method, the majority opinion is taken *after* the proposals are aggregated for each representative. The doctrinal paradox arises when these two methods of interpreting representatives' votes lead to conflicting outcomes. In particular, the goal-driven interpretation may reveal parliamentary support for reaching the policy goal, whereas the proposal-driven interpretation may lead to a policy program that fails to reach the policy goal. This occurs solely because a different way of interpreting representatives' preferences is used and not because their preferences have changed.[28]

Consider the instance of the doctrinal paradox as presented in Table 6.1.[29] Imagine a legislature consisting of three representatives (three MPs or three political parties). In this instance, we assume that the policy goal is reached if *at least one* legislative proposal is accepted. That is, we say that a representative (an MP/political party) intends to reach the policy goal if it accepts at least one legislative proposal. Similarly, a policy program is sufficient with respect to the policy goal if it implements at least one legislative proposal. As

Table 6.1 The Doctrinal Paradox

	Diesel taxes	*Nuclear power plants*	*Insulating social housing*	Goal-driven outcome
Representative 1	Yes	No	No	Yes
Representative 2	No	Yes	No	Yes
Representative 3	No	No	Yes	Yes
Proposal-driven outcome	No	No	No	Yes / No

the relation between accepted legislative proposals is one of logical disjunction (proposal 1 *or* proposal 2 *or* proposal 3 is accepted), such an instance of the doctrinal paradox is sometimes referred to as the *disjunctive doctrinal paradox*.[30]

Table 6.1 shows the dichotomous (yes or no) preferences of three representatives on each of the legislative proposals. On the basis of these preferences, we can determine whether a majority in parliament intends to reach the policy goal of a 49% reduction in greenhouse gas emissions. Taking a proposal-driven interpretation of the representatives' preferences in Table 6.1 results in a policy program that does not reach the policy goal, as none of the legislative proposals is accepted by a majority in parliament. For example, the proposal to put a heftier tax on diesel is rejected by representatives 2 and 3, constituting a two-third majority. Similarly, the proposals to build nuclear power plants and to introduce subsidies for insulating social housing are rejected by a two-third majority. As none of the proposals is accepted, the policy goal is not reached.

However, if we take a goal-driven interpretation of the representatives' preferences, we see that a majority in parliament intends to reach the policy goal. In the disjunctive doctrinal paradox, the policy goal is reached when at least one proposal is accepted. Given that representatives 1, 2, and 3 each support at least one legislative proposal, they arrive at a policy program that is sufficient to reach the policy goal. Since the MPs/political parties 1, 2, and 3 form a majority (even unanimity) in parliament, we can conclude from a goal-driven interpretation that a majority in parliament intends to reach the policy goal.

The doctrinal paradox impairs the legislative capacity for action with respect to policy goals leading to deficits in democratic decision-making. Can this problem be resolved? Legislatures tend to vote on policy proposals but, since this may lead to inaction with respect to policy goals that the majority endorses, one may wonder whether the proposal-driven method should be replaced by a goal-driven method of voting. This option, however, would be unfeasible. In order to go the goal-driven way, it would not do to vote for or against a policy goal: given that (a) the policy goal could be reached by different combinations of legislative proposals and (b) none of these combinations is determined in advance of the vote, the representatives would need to determine by means of which combination of legislative proposals this goal is to be implemented. In these circumstances, going the goal-driven way would be combinatorially problematic, as it means that legislators would possibly have to cast a lot of votes in order to decide on the policy program toward reaching a given policy goal.

Consider the two procedures by which the goal-driven method can be implemented. The first procedure would have parliament vote on all possible policy programs. The second procedure would have parliament vote in two stages: representatives first cast a vote on whether to accept the policy goal or not. Then, if parliament supports the policy goal, representatives vote on all the possible policy programs to implement that goal. In the case of the disjunctive doctrinal paradox presented in Table 6.1, both procedures would have parliament cast 8 votes. The first procedure would have parliament vote on each possible policy program and with 3 policy proposals, there are $\binom{3}{0}+\binom{3}{1}+\binom{3}{2}+\binom{3}{3}=8$ possible policy programs.[31] The second procedure would have parliament first vote on the goal and, if the goal is accepted, on the 7 policy programs that reach the policy goal (all programs in which at least one proposal is accepted). With 3 policy proposals, both procedures require parliament to cast more votes than it would have to cast in a proposal-driven practice, and this number of votes significantly increases with each additional legislative proposal.[32]

Given the impracticality involved in multiplying the number of votes to determine a policy program toward reaching one policy goal, the goal-driven way is unfeasible. The least time-consuming way to have representatives in parliament translate policy goals into legislation is to let them vote in a proposal-driven rather than in a goal-driven way, that is, to let them vote on each possible legislative proposal instead of on full programs.[33] However, as this decision-making method is likely to inhibit the legislative capacity to reach policy goals, we propose another way to fix this problem in the remainder of this chapter.

6.4 Tactical voting

We submit that tactical voting, embedded in procedures of deliberation and bargaining, plays a key role in fixing parliamentary failures to reach policy goals that are caused by a paradoxical distribution of votes. In order to reverse the paradoxical distribution of votes once it occurs, and to have parliament implement a policy program that is sufficient to achieve a policy goal, representatives should be able to adjust their votes in light of the consequence that their votes have for reaching the desired policy goal. For example, in the doctrinal paradox presented in Table 6.1, representative 1 could cast a tactical vote in favor of nuclear power plants in order to ensure that at least one policy proposal is accepted and, thus, that a policy program is implemented that reaches the policy goal of reducing greenhouse gas emissions by 49%.[34]

Providing representatives with the opportunity to adjust their votes when facing a doctrinal paradox requires introducing a second round of voting. For the second, tactical, round of voting to achieve the policy goal, representatives should know how to change their votes given the anticipated votes of others and the desired outcome. For this reason, the second round of voting should be preceded by a round of deliberation and bargaining regarding their voting strategies.

Our proposal aligns with the approach defended by John Ferejohn, who argues that overcoming the doctrinal paradox of gridlock to legislative decision-making requires that representatives reconsider their votes in a round of deliberation.[35] Ferejohn presents the re-adjustment of votes as a matter of legislators' duty to prevent enactment of bad laws:

> [M]embers of collective bodies [legislatures-DM] may have duties to choose how to vote in light of the possible coherence of the resulting policies that will be produced. They may have duties, that is, to adjust their votes . . . in the course of deliberation, in order to make the pattern of their collective decisions cohere.[36]

For our purposes, it suffices to say that creating an institutional setting that enables legislators to adjust their vote in the course of deliberation is dictated by the democratic values at stake in restoring the legislative capacity for action.

In the next section, we argue that the second round of deliberation and voting will not resolve the paradoxical distribution of votes unless it takes place behind closed doors. Before turning to this argument, we address two challenges against tactical voting that Ferejohn identifies: first, tactical voting can be seen as "deceptive" and, second, it may be subject to coordination problems.[37]

6.4.1 Is tactical voting deceptive?

Creating space for voting Yes or No on the same issue is inviting political actors to submit voting preferences that do not reflect their genuine judgments regarding the issue at hand. Such misrepresentation of voting preferences may be a source of concern insofar as it is a common assumption that political actors ought to express sincere beliefs and commitments in their votes; voting other than in the way one believes is considered insincere and, thus, morally objectionable. Tactical behavior appears unprincipled in a similar way as making concessions to one's position for the sake of compromise does. In both cases, the specter of being judged a "flip-flopper" may make legislators reluctant to adopt this strategy.

The objection to tactical voting loses some of its force if we acknowledge that one may express her preference for a given legislative proposal and also explain, appealing to the very same reasons, why she will not vote for it.[38] This justification is particularly strong in situations of interdependent choice of which voting is an example: an individual vote does not directly determine the outcome but contributes to the outcome only given the choices of others. In this context, voting for one's most preferred legislative proposal is not always the best way to bring about the policy goal. As the examples discussed earlier illustrate, voting one's genuine preferences regarding specific legislative proposals may get one further away from the policy goal one favors rather than bring one closer to it. To be required to vote for one's genuine preferences in such a situation would be to defend a lost cause. Given that the final outcome depends on a combination of aggregated choices, the only way to reduce the likelihood that the collective decision will be the outcome one disfavors would be to anticipate the choices of others and to adjust one's own voting choice in such a way that one's vote reduces the chance of arriving at the collective decision one least prefers. From this perspective, Keith Dowding and Martin van Hees argue that tactical voting is pursuing one's beliefs and commitments taking feasibility conditions into account. If this is manipulation, they say, it is "sincere manipulation."[39] As long as a tactical vote decreases the likelihood that the final decision fails to reach the policy goal that constituents support, it can be justified in terms of the same reasons that drive people's preferences regarding policy goals.

6.4.2 Is tactical voting subject to collective action problems?

A further objection to the tactical voting argument is that it is not always clear that a tactical vote actually does increase the likelihood that the collective decision reaches the desired outcome, that is, induces a policy program that reaches the desired policy goal. For instance, a situation may arise in which strategic votes *cancel each other out*. As Jon Elster argues: "[I]f a second voter anticipates strategic voting by the first and counteracts that move by misrepresenting *his* preferences, he can bring about the outcome that would have occurred if both had voted sincerely."[40] This is problematic, because it calls into question our claim that tactical voting will break the legislative gridlock and increase the likelihood that the collective decision reaches the policy goal.

Whereas the canceling out of votes may obstruct the possibility of reaching the desired outcome through tactical voting in general, this objection does not hold for tactical voting when it is used to eliminate the distribution of votes with the structure of the doctrinal paradox. The doctrinal paradox is characterized by an inconsistency between the goal-driven majority judgment and the proposal-driven majority judgment. In our presentation of the (disjunctive) doctrinal paradox (see Table 6.1), there is always a majority in parliament in favor of reaching the policy goal, while there is no majority of representatives in favor of any policy proposal toward reaching that goal. Since a majority is needed to accept a policy proposal, the majority of representatives who intend to reach the policy goal can ensure that the goal is reached independently of the (tactical) votes of other representatives by simply all accepting at least two policy proposals toward reaching the policy goal. Thus, in instances of the doctrinal paradox, the danger of tactical votes canceling each other out is not present, as representatives who are part of the majority in support of the policy goal can submit a tactical vote that reaches the policy goal.

Now, we can grant that this is the case but still wonder whether this strategy always works. Adjusting votes in order to reach the desired policy goal may be subject to collective action problems. For one, as Ferejohn observes, given that each representative should be open to reconsidering their vote in light of the votes by others and the desired outcome and given that there are many possible deliberatively stable patterns of adjusted votes that may bring about the desired policy goal, legislators may face a problem of settling on one pattern rather than another. If they rank different distributions of tactical votes equally, they confront a coordination problem.[41] If representatives rank different distributions of tactical votes differently, they create a game environment in which different equilibria are possible, some of which may have the structure of the bargaining game or the Prisoner's Dilemma. Whether the policy goal will be realized depends on whether they will be able to resolve such collective action problems.

That they will indeed be able to resolve them is supported by the following considerations. First, voting is embedded in patterns of deliberation and bargaining, which make it possible for legislators to negotiate on tactical votes, also across clusters of legislative proposals in different policy areas. Second, the representatives care more about reaching the policy goal than about the specific policies to implement it – this assumption is inherent in the description of a legislative incapacity to reach policy goals as an instance of the doctrinal paradox. Third, they are involved in repeated interactions which, from the perspective of their parliamentary interactions, are spread over an indeterminate time. Game theory demonstrates that the presence of these factors in a game environment should suffice to coordinate in an equilibrium.[42] Various domestic and international policy areas are rich in illustrations of correcting or preventing the bargaining game and Prisoner's Dilemma situations,[43] and there is no reason to exclude them in the context of parliamentary politics.

6.5 Secrecy and tactical voting

In the preceding sections, we have argued that when parliamentary voting runs into a collective decision-making problem with the structure of the doctrinal paradox, the legislative capacity to act and reach policy goals is frustrated, leading to deficits in democratic decision-making. We argued, like Ferejohn, that in order to restore the legislative capacity to act, legislators ought to adjust their votes in the course of deliberation and bargaining aiming, in the second voting round, to arrive at a distribution of votes that realizes the policy goals. We argued that tactical voting need not (1) be insincere nor (2) misfire due to collective action problems. In this section, we argue that this way of restoring the legislative capacity to act requires that the second round of deliberation and voting takes place in a closed-door institutional setting.

Our claim to this effect rests on two pillars. First, along with recent developments in democratic theory, we present voting as intertwined with deliberation. Second, insofar as voting is intertwined with deliberation, we argue that the same reasons that support moving deliberation behind closed doors apply to voting. Our argument is also similarly qualified: just as secrecy of deliberation does not apply to legislative deliberation across the board, so secrecy of voting does not apply to legislative voting across the board. Given that legislatures, among all branches of government, have the unique democratic role to, as Warren and Mansbridge put it, "enable two-way communication between constituents and representatives,"[44] openness of parliamentary decision-making is of particular importance. Accordingly, we do not advocate abandoning open voting but, rather, defend a two-stage process in which an open vote is followed by a secret vote *if functionally necessary to overcome a paradoxical distribution of votes*.

A recent turn in democratic scholarship presents voting as embedded in patterns of deliberation and bargaining. This idea marks a departure from the long tradition that saw deliberation and voting as opposed to each other, reflecting the opposition between aggregative and deliberative models of democracy. Initially, the idea that deliberation and voting belong together rather than oppose each other was motivated by the acknowledgment of what deliberation may accomplish for voting.[45] Most recently, the reverse argument has gained traction emphasizing the way that voting benefits deliberation. In this context, voting has been seen as a communication device and, as such, interwoven with deliberation.[46] Alfred Moore and Kieran O'Doherty argue that a voting outcome may communicate, first, that a group has taken a collective stance on an issue and is ready to move on, in which case voting is a closure mechanism of deliberation. Second, it may indicate points of disagreement that prevent a group from arriving at a desired outcome on an issue. In this case, voting communicates a need for further deliberation.

In the case under discussion, a voting outcome may communicate that a group has adopted a collective position on a policy program toward reaching a policy goal, in which case the vote closes deliberation. Alternatively, it may reveal a paradoxical distribution of votes. In the latter case, the vote communicates that while there is the initial "deliberative acceptance"[47] of policy goals, there is disagreement on the specific policies to implement these goals. In revealing a paradoxical distribution of votes, which inhibits the realization of policy goals, the vote communicates that further deliberation is needed and it focuses deliberation on possible patterns of vote adjustment by way of resolving disagreement.

To see voting not simply as a decision-making device but as a communication device intertwined with deliberation is to see it as vulnerable to similar problems as those that pertain to deliberation, one of which is the negative impact of publicity on the processes of deliberation. As explained in Section 6.1, deliberative democrats recognize that public deliberation is deliberation with an eye to how outside parties will judge representatives' behavior. By introducing an audience, publicity makes legislators play to the gallery whereby they behave in accordance with the supposed constituents' expectations. For fear of falling into disfavor with the electorate, publicity makes them reluctant to shift their positions and change their minds even in light of better arguments. Just as public deliberation is deliberation with an eye on how outside parties will judge representatives' behavior, so can public voting be seen as voting with an eye to how outside parties will judge their behavior. The fear of falling into disgrace with their electorate is likewise likely to prevent legislators from deliberatively reconsidering and changing their votes even if the adjusted votes lead to a better outcome under the circumstances.

Our case study well illustrates the way in which deliberation and voting and the settings in which each is conducted are interwoven. Resolving the doctrinal paradox, we argued with Ferejohn, requires legislators to deliberatively re-adjust their votes. For reasons laid out in Section 6.1, having legislators deliberate and bargain about changing their voting choices in open settings is likely to fail. Closed-door settings are more conducive to them revising their positions. Note, however, that the positive effect of closed-door deliberation may be forgone if the vote meant to bring it to a close is subsequently held in open settings. Given the negative impact of publicity, legislators could be less inclined to cast an open vote that communicates a change of mind regarding their voting strategies. Alternatively, expecting to vote in open settings, they could be unwilling to adjust their position in light of the desired outcome in the preceding deliberations, obstructing the advantages that closed-door deliberations are supposed to provide. In either case, open voting settings stand in the way of the positive impact that closed-door deliberations can have on the outcome of a decision-making process. Similarly, given the negative impact of publicity, open deliberation settings may not enable voters to reflect on their preferences in a way conducive to voting behind closed doors.

In the face of a deliberative impasse inhibiting the legislative capacity to act, democratic scholars recommend moving legislative deliberation behind closed doors. Likewise, we argue that in the face of voting deadlocks, legislative voting should be moved behind closed doors: closed-door settings eliminate the factors that make legislators reluctant to change their vote just as they eliminate the factors that make them reluctant to change their mind. Eliminating concerns about what the public would say, closed-door deliberation makes legislators freer to reconsider their views if they realize that sticking to their arguments will not lead to achieving the policy goals. In a similar way, voting behind closed doors removes distorting incentives that prevent them from adjusting their votes and averting a deadlock.[48]

We have argued that accepting that deliberation and voting are intertwined commits us to accepting that publicity affects both processes in a similar way and gives us reason to move them both behind closed doors. Even if one grants this reasoning, one could resist the idea of a dual open-then-secret sequence of deliberation and voting regime we propose. One could argue that the dual procedure is flawed because it is difficult to explain the value of the open sequence of deliberation and vote once the value of a successive closed-door sequence has been established. If the open- and closed-door settings yield the same outcome, the objection goes, the open round could be considered otiose. If the two settings yield a different outcome, the open round could be dismissed as based on potentially false judgments. In effect, it could be argued that our proposal amounts to a defense of closed-door settings *simpliciter*.[49]

Our proposal for a dual open-then-secret deliberation and voting regime avoids this objection. From the perspective of our argument, the open voting round is not redundant. In an open-then-closed deliberation and voting regime, the function of the open vote is to determine and communicate whether deliberation has come to an end. If no paradoxical distribution of votes has been identified, the open vote marks a closure of deliberation. If a paradoxical pattern of votes is revealed, the open vote communicates a need for further deliberation in the course of which the representatives reconsider their voting strategy and cast adjusted votes. Thus, the dual-track procedure has a heuristic function of identifying the presence of potential paradoxes and creating incentives for better deliberations, which can help MPs vote in such a way as to achieve policy goals the second time round.[50]

6.6 Accountability of representatives

We have said so far that (1) tactical voting reinstates the legislative capacity to act in reaching policy goals in situations in which collective decision-making runs into a collective decision-making paradox such as the doctrinal paradox and that (2) secrecy creates conditions for tactical voting. Accepting (1) and (2) commits us to accepting the claim that (3) in the non-trivial set of conditions specified in this chapter, to ensure parliamentary capacity to act, collective decision-making mechanisms must make room for a round of closed-door deliberation and voting following the open round. The legislative assembly's authority to resort to secrecy takes normative effect when secrecy is functionally necessary.

To this argument, the objection can be raised that the secret stage of the dual deliberation and voting procedure impedes mechanisms of democratic accountability. Secrecy conceals representatives' deliberation and voting patterns, thus placing them beyond their constituents' scrutiny. When policy goals fail or half-hearted action is taken toward problems that were meant to be resolved by the legislature, secrecy makes it impossible to hold representatives to account: to voice objections, demand a change, or call upon to initiate amendments. In order to ensure democratic accountability, secrecy, the objection holds, should be abandoned.

The strength of the objection depends on the form of democratic representation it presupposes and a corresponding accountability mechanism. Traditionally, political representation is spelled out in terms of the principal-agent relation, in which legislators (agents) receive their mandate from citizens (principals) through elections. The content of their mandate is determined by electoral promises. The representatives-agents are called to account by the citizens-principals for the extent to which they have realized their electoral promises in their term in office, hence, we speak of "promissory representation."[51]

Besides this traditional form of political representation, empirical political scientists have described two alternative forms of representation: anticipatory and gyroscopic representation.[52] Unlike "promissory representation," in "anticipatory representation" citizens do not punish or reward representatives for how well they have realized the interests they promised to realize at the moment citizens installed them in office. Instead, citizens consider the interests they happen to have at the time of the new election round when they decide about the renewal of their office-term. Accordingly, representatives, when in office, take actions that they anticipate their electorate will reward in the next election. They, thus, represent not the citizens who installed them in office at previous elections but the future citizens who will decide about the renewal of their term in office in the next election round; hence, "anticipatory representation."[53] By contrast, in "gyroscopic representation" – defended, among others, by Jane Mansbridge – citizens select representatives based on predictions that they will act in office in ways approved by the citizens without being monitored and controlled.[54] Legislators are presumed to have a built-in policy-making compass toward the goals citizens want to have advanced. Being selected on the grounds of their internal motivation to further citizens' interests, the representatives are granted discretion to act autonomously when in office.

In his insightful discussion of the question whether closed-door legislative decision-making inhibits accountability of the legislators, Kogelmann argues that, with the exception of "promissory representation," other forms of political representation can reconcile accountability with secrecy regarding legislators' deliberation and voting patterns in office.[55] Neither in "anticipatory representation" nor in "gyroscopic representation" do mechanisms of accountability target the office-performance of representatives. What matters in "anticipatory representation" are only the changes in citizens' welfare, measured by the advancement of their interests at the time of a new election round, not what legislators did in office. Similarly, "gyroscopic representation" is compatible with secrecy because citizens are fairly sure that representatives installed in office will pursue citizens' interests for moral and internal reasons.[56] Knowing what policies they are likely to support, there is no need to monitor what office holders do in office and, consequently, office holders are granted full decision-making discretion. The accountability mechanism, as Kogelmann puts it, "does not operate *while* the candidate is in office but *before*."[57] Moreover, in "gyroscopic representation," a strong internal commitment to the mandate attached to their office creates "horizontal" accountability ties between representatives to the effect that they monitor and sanction the behavior of each other and keep each other to the requirements of their mandate.[58]

According to Kogelmann, only "promissory representation" resists secrecy of legislative decision-making. This is because in order to determine whether representatives have acted in the way they promised, citizens must know how they performed *viz*. deliberated and voted in office. This, however, requires disclosure of their deliberation and voting patterns. According to Kogelmann, "secrecy will often make it impossible to determine whether politicians have made good on their promises."[59] Next, contrary to Kogelmann, we argue that even the model of accountability assumed in "promissory representation" allows for a degree of secrecy in governance.

Traditionally, the principal-agent model underpinning the promissory form of political representation spans a spectrum marked by two models at its outer edges *viz*. the delegate and the trustee models.[60] As delegates, agents are bound by the instructions from the principals. Being a mere transmission device of the constituents' preferences, agents have no decision-making discretion and are called to account for how closely their performance conveys the principals' preferences. At the opposite edge of the spectrum are agents as trustees. In this role, agents are free to act as seems best to them in pursuit of their principals' interests; they are called to account only for the results they reach.

The delegate model requires more transparency than the trustee model. In the delegate model, given that the agents are called to account for how well their actions reproduce the principals' preferences, it is crucial that principals receive in real time information to assess the agents' performance, such as the way they argue and vote, during the decision-making process. In the trustee model, principals evaluate the agents only in terms of the results they achieve, hence, transparency of results will be required. To the extent that it is less relevant how the agents arrived at the results, transparency about the details of the decision-making process is less relevant.

Mansbridge's distinction between "transparency-in-process" and "transparency-in-rationale"[61] can be usefully employed to describe how the scope of transparency owed to citizens-principals changes as we move between these two ends of the spectrum. The delegate model of political representation requires transparency in process *viz.* citizens' access to the details of the representatives' performance in the legislative process. The trustee model requires only transparency-in-rationale *viz.* citizens' access only to the reasons on which representatives' decisions are based rather than to the process through which they are taken. This form of transparency is less encompassing, and it is compatible with higher levels of opacity. Thus, depending on the model used to describe the principal-agent relation, the object of accountability and the corresponding claim to access state information will differ accordingly: as one moves from the delegate model toward the trustee model of the principal-agent relation, the room for secrecy in legislative decision-making becomes larger.[62]

Based on the argument above, secrecy poses a problem to representatives' accountability only in the delegate model of the "promissory" form of political representation. Here accountability requires disclosure of the process leading to formulating a policy program that implements or fails to implement policy goals. It thus requires disclosure of representatives' deliberation and voting patterns. Does secrecy prevent attribution of accountability in this case?

Note, first, that arriving at a policy program that implements the policy goal is a matter of collective action and, thus, that we are talking here of accountability for an outcome of collective action. In order to determine whether secrecy prevents representatives' accountability for reaching policy outcomes, we need to determine the sense in which members of a collective can be held individually accountable for an outcome of collective action.

In answering this question, we draw on the existing discussion about individual responsibility for collective outcomes. There are two dominant models of attributing responsibility for a collective outcome to the individual members of a collective: (a) we can attribute *equal* responsibility to individual members, or (b) we can attribute responsibility in *proportion* to how each member contributed to the collective outcome.[63] If we adopt the equal distribution model, secrecy does not inhibit attributing responsibility to individual members of the collective. This is because equal attribution of responsibility does not require attending to how distinct members of the collective contributed to it: irrespective of individual contribution, each representative is responsible to the same degree. Extrapolating this reasoning to the problem of accountability, we submit that secrecy does not inhibit calling individual members of the collective – MPs or distinct political parties – to account for reaching policy goals. Given that each representative is accountable to the same degree, the fact that secrecy conceals the voting choices of representatives is not an obstruction to holding them accountable because the information that the secrecy conceals is irrelevant to their accountability.

Secrecy inhibits the attribution of individual responsibility of representatives only if we adopt the model of proportional distribution of responsibility. Here, determining the degree to which each member of the collective is responsible for failing to reach policy goals would require a complex calculation, *viz.* verifying whether their particular vote was pivotal to the collective failure, but no such calculation can get off the ground as long as secrecy conceals the voting patterns. Now, the impossibility of holding representatives responsible does not necessarily imply that responsibility is impossible. With regard to the outcomes of collective action, responsibility can be fleshed out either in terms of individual responsibility of group members and/or in terms of collective responsibility of the group.[64] Extrapolating this to the discussion on accountability, we could then argue that, in the situation in which a closed-door deliberation and voting stage is functionally necessary to protect the legislative capacity to act, accountability for the legislative decision can be borne by the assembly as a collective body. Secrecy does not pose a problem to holding it to account as a collective because it does not conceal the action of the collective. With regard to this idea, however, one could be concerned that holding the parliament to account as a collective would be unfeasible. The following response may be appealing. As Holly Lawford-Smith argues, a collective is a group of members related to one another in terms of hierarchy and role responsibilities, in which case holding the collective to account entails holding its members to account according to their roles.[65] In the case of parliament, holding the collective to account would involve holding representatives as *members* to account. In this case, given the equal rank of all members, collective accountability would be the same as in the equal distribution model of accountability. Hence, as we have seen earlier, secrecy does not impede the attribution of accountability.

6.7 Conclusion

In this chapter, we have argued that the preservation of the legislative capacity to act is among the conditions under which the political authority of democratic assembly to resort to secrecy takes normative effect. We have shown that legislative decision-making may run into collective decision problems with the structure of the doctrinal paradox. If this is the case, the legislative capacity to reach policy goals is frustrated, leading to deficits in democratic governance. We have suggested a dual open-then-secret deliberation and voting procedure to address this problem. Our argument draws on the claim, defended by deliberative democrats, that closed-door democratic deliberations are justified if they enhance the quality of legislative deliberation in the face of legislative gridlocks. Presenting voting as intertwined with deliberation, we have extended this argument to parliamentary voting. Our argument does not defend closed-door voting across the board. Nonetheless, the proposal for a closed-door deliberation and voting sequence following, *if needed*, an open one qualifies the prevailing view that parliamentary voting should be public.

Notes

1 Co-authored with Suzanne Bloks.
2 Warren and Mansbridge 2016, 87.
3 Warren and Mansbridge 2016, 87, 141.
4 Cohen 1997, 76–77; Dryzek 2000; Gutmann and Thompson 1996, 126–127; Benhabib 1996.
5 Chambers 2004; Lee 2019.
6 Kogelmann 2021 is an exception.
7 Moore and O'Doherty 2014; Serota and O'Doherty 2022; Chambers and Warren 2023.
8 Deliberation is traditionally understood as a decision-making process aiming at a consensus. There is disagreement about whether deliberation and compromise go hand in hand: some authors think that deliberation can also aim at reaching a fair compromise (Warren and Mansbridge 2016), whereas others argue that deliberation and compromise are distinct projects (O'Flynn and Setälä 2020). While we have no space to engage in this debate, we use the term "deliberation" also to refer to a compromise-focused decision-making process.
9 Elster 1998; Chambers 2004.
10 Habermas 1996, 179.
11 Snowe 2013, 27.
12 Gutmann and Thompson 2012.
13 Gutmann and Thompson 2012, 150.
14 Cited after Warren and Mansbridge 2016, 107.
15 Kogelmann 2021, 66.
16 Warren and Mansbridge 2016, 87. Baume and Novak 2020 qualify these findings arguing that in cultures that value compromise, these effects may be weaker.
17 Kaminski 2005, 11.
18 Council Legal Service 1994, cited after Baume and Novak 2020, 79.
19 Ulbert and Risse 2005, 40.
20 Warren and Mansbridge 2016, 108; Chambers 2004.
21 Kogelmann 2021.
22 Kogelmann 2021, 212.
23 Kogelmann 2021, 6.
24 This name is due to legal scholars who focused on a version arising in a court of law, see Kornhauser and Sager 1986. Pettit (2001) demonstrates the relevance of the paradox in democratic theory in which context it is often referred to as a *discursive dilemma*.
25 In relation to legislative voting, the doctrinal paradox has been discussed by Ferejohn (2007) and Ottonelli (2010) among others.
26 See the EU energy union strategy published on 25–02–2015 (https://ec.europa.eu/energy/topics/energy-strategy/energy-union_en?redir=1#content-heading-2 (accessed 26–11–2020)). Another example of the doctrinal paradox could be protecting a natural habitat as a national park by (a) allowing it to further develop its unique biodiversity (ecological reason), (b) promoting it as a place of religious significance (religious reason), and (c) attracting ecotourists (economic reason) (List 2006, 368). For yet other

examples, see Ferejohn 2007, 138–140 (addressing an external security threat by setting up a new agency with powers to interfere with certain rights or interests) and Ferejohn 2012, 99–100 (reforming economic security program).

27 "Proposal-driven" and "goal-driven" methods refer to what in the literature on the topic are also labeled "premise-based" and "conclusion-based" methods.

28 To recognize the occurrence of a doctrinal paradox, it may be necessary to cluster legislative proposals, each targeting the same policy goal, in the same voting round. A round of deliberation and bargaining preceding voting can contribute to the clustering of policy proposals. Clustering is practiced in majoritarian systems (e.g., the Australian Senate) and its advantages have also been recognized – if not always implemented – in consensual democracies. In the Netherlands, for instance, where clustering of legislative proposals has been on the political agenda for some time, Cabinet Rutte III agreed in the coalition agreement on the reform of the tax system. Toward this long-term policy goal, a cluster of legislative proposals has been proposed to reduce the tax payable by individuals, to abolish dividend taxes and keep taxes low for international enterprises. In some parliaments, for example, the European Parliament, committees cluster proposals on the basis of policy areas. See, for example, www.europarl.europa.eu/cmsdata/committees/booklet/Committees-quick-look-EN-web.pdf

29 The paradox originates in the field of judgment aggregation (see, e.g., List and Puppe 2009). We present the paradox in a social choice theory framework, as we are concerned with the aggregation of voting preferences.

30 The *disjunctive* doctrinal paradox should be distinguished from the *conjunctive* doctrinal paradox in which the relation between accepted proposals is one of logical conjunction (proposal 1 *and* proposal 2 *and* proposal 3 are accepted), that is, the policy goal is reached if *every* policy proposal is accepted.

31 That is, one program that implements none of the proposals, three programs consisting of only 1 proposal; three programs consisting of 2 proposals; and one program that implements all of the proposals.

32 The number of possible policy programs doubles with each additional policy proposal: It increases to 1+4+6+4+1=16 with 4 policy proposals, to 1+5+10+10+5+1=32 with 5 policy proposals and to 1+6+15+20+15+6+1=64 with 6 policy proposals.

33 Whereas our argument for the proposal-driven method is empirical, it is common in the literature to make a normative argument in favor of a premise-driven way. The normative argument presents premises as reasons for adopting/rejecting a collective decision. It subsequently addresses the (in)consistency between the premises and the outcome of the collective decision in terms of collective rationality: See Pettit 2001. Given that legislative proposals are not reasons for parliaments to adopt the policy goals but instruments to reach policy goals, the collective decision problem we address is better described in terms of collective efficiency rather than collective rationality.

34 Is tactical voting the only path forward? One may suggest that a distribution of labor might be made between plenary and committee sessions to elaborate better compromises to further overarching goals. This overlooks the fact that committee decision-making, too, is vulnerable to doctrinal paradoxes.

35 Ferejohn 2007, 2012. Resolving voting paradoxes by deliberation has been defended by some, for example, Cohen 1997; Ferejohn 2012. Dryzek and List (2003) argue that deliberation can relax the conditions of the Arrow and Gibbard-Satterthwaite impossibility theorems, making meaningful decisions possible. It has been questioned by others, for example, Ottonelli 2010, 680–681.

36 Ferejohn 2007, 125–126.

37 Ferejohn 2007, 135, and 137.

38 Elster 2015, 82.

39 Dowding and Van Hees 2008.

40 Elster 2013, 74.
41 Ferejohn 2007, 137.
42 See, for example, Schelling 1960 (coordination problem); Axelrod and Hamilton 1981 (Prisoner's Dilemma); Lau and Mui 2008 (Battle of Sexes).
43 Parisi and Ghey 2003.
44 Warren and Mansbridge 2016, 89.
45 Goodin 2008; Fishkin 2018 argue that deliberation enables voters to acquire a better understanding of their own and others' interests and values in such a way that voting results are more likely to reflect both individual preferences and collective preferences.
46 Moore and O'Doherty 2014; Serota and O'Doherty 2022; Chambers and Warren 2023.
47 Moore and O'Doherty 2014, 304.
48 Whereas we recognize that there may be methods to have representatives strategize their votes other than by means of closed-door voting (such as the whipping endorsed in majoritarian systems), we propose secret voting as a new element to be added to the existing repertoire, an option to be used when the other options turn out to be ineffective (as the Brexit negotiations demonstrated, the whips' power to impose specific voting strategies on MPs may weaken).
49 This objection is modeled on the objection raised by Vermeule (2015, 220) against a two stage open-then-secret voting regime proposed by Bentham. In "Political Tactics" Bentham claims that in order to protect legislators from "the influence of a particular interest opposed to the public interest" the legislature should adopt sequential open and secret voting on the same issue with the outcome of the secret vote trumping the outcome of the open vote (1999, 146). Our proposal bears a similarity to Bentham's but avoids Vermeule's objection as we explain later.
50 One may object that the secrecy in the second deliberation and voting round has no real function, because citizens may be able to reconstruct how the representatives adjusted their votes by comparing the votes in the open round with the outcome of the tactical vote behind closed doors. However, the complexity of decision-making involving multiple proposals in which it is possible that votes for and against certain legislative proposals cancel each other out would make it impossible for voters to determine which representatives changed their vote and how.
51 Mansbridge 2003.
52 For an overview, see Mansbridge 2003. Mansbridge also mentions "surrogate representation," which is representation by a representative with whom one has no electoral relationship. As we focus on representation by elected representatives, we do not discuss this form of representation.
53 Mansbridge 2003.
54 Mansbridge 2009.
55 Kogelmann 2021.
56 Mansbridge 2003, 520.
57 Kogelmann 2021, 61. Emphasis in the original.
58 Mansbridge 2009, 384–386.
59 Kogelmann 2021, 59.
60 Pitkin 1967.
61 Mansbridge 2009, 385–386.
62 Cf. Da Silveira 2003.
63 Pasternak 2010.
64 Pettit 2007; Lawford-Smith 2019.
65 Lawford-Smith 2019, 147–158.

Bibliography

Adams, N.P. (2017). In defense of content-independence. *Legal Theory* 23(3), 143–167.

Agamben, G. (2005). *State of Exception*. University of Chicago Press.

Aldrich, R. & Richterova, D. (2018). Ambient accountability: Intelligence services in Europe and the decline of state secrecy. *West European Politics* 41(4), 1003–1024.

Alloa, E. (2018). Transparency: A magic concept of modernity. In E. Alloa & D. Thomä (Eds.), *Transparency, Society and Subjectivity: Critical Perspectives*. Palgrave MacMillan.

Anechiarico, F. & Jacobs, J.B. (1996). *The Pursuit of Absolute Integrity: How Corruption Control Makes Government Ineffective*. University of Chicago Press.

Aquinas, T. (1485/1999). *Summa Theologica*. Penguin Classics.

Arneson, R.J. (2003). Defending the purely instrumental account of democratic legitimacy. *Journal of Political Philosophy* 11(1), 122–132.

Axelrod, R. & Hamilton, W. (1981). The evolution of cooperation. *Science* 211, 1390–1396.

Bauhr, M. & Grimes, M. (2014). Indignation or resignation: The implications of transparency for societal accountability. *Governance* 27(2), 291–320.

Baume, S. & Novak, S. (2020). Compromise and publicity in democracy: An ambiguous relationship. In S. Baume & S. Novak (Eds.), *Compromises in Democracy: Palgrave Studies in Compromise after Conflict*. Palgrave Macmillan, 69–94.

Baume, S. & Papadopoulos, Y. (2018). Transparency: From Bentham's inventory of virtuous effects to contemporary evidence-based skepticism. *Critical Review of International Social and Political Philosophy* 21(2), 2018.

Benhabib, S. (Ed). (1996). *Democracy and Difference: Contesting the Boundaries of the Political*. Princeton University Press.

Benhabib, S. (2011). *Dignity in Adversity: Human Rights in Troubled Times*. Polity Press.

Benkler, Y. (2014). A public accountability defense for national security leakers and whistleblowers. *Harvard Law and Policy Review* 8, 281–326.

Benn, S.I. & Gaus, G.F. (1983). *Public and Private in Social Life*. St. Martin's Press.

Bentham, J. (1843). *The Works of Jeremy Bentham*. William Tait.

Bentham, J. (1999). *Political Tactics: The Collected Works of Jeremy Bentham*. M. James, C. Blamires, C. Pease-Watkin (Eds.). Clarendon Press.

Besson, S. (2014). Human rights and constitutional law: Patterns of mutual validation and legitimation. In R. Cruft, M. Liao, & M. Renzo (Eds.), *Philosophical Foundations of Human Rights*. Oxford University Press, 279–287.

Birkinshaw, P. (2006). Transparency as a human right. In C. Hood & D. Heald (Eds.), *Transparency: The Key to Better Governance?* Oxford University Press, 189–191.

Bloustein, E. (1977). Group privacy: The right to huddle. *Rutgers-Camden Law Journal* 8, 219–283.

Bodei, R. (2011). From secrecy to transparency: Reason of state and democracy. *Philosophy and Social Criticism* 37(8): 889–898.

Bodnar, A. & Pudzianowska, D. (2010). Alleged existence of secret CIA facilities on polish territory in search of truth and accountability. In M. Nowak & R. Schmidt (Eds.), *Extraordinary Renditions and the Protection of Human Rights*. Boltzmann Institute of Human Rights, 79–98.

Bohman, J. & Rehg, W. (Eds.). (1997). *Deliberative Democracy: Essays on Reason and Politics*. MIT Press.

Bok, S. (1984). *Secrets: On the Ethics of Concealment and Revelation*. Vintage Books.

Boot, E. (2019a). Leaks and the limits of press freedom. *Ethical Theory Moral Practice* 22(2), 483–500.

Boot, E. (2019b). *The Ethics of Whistleblowing*. Routledge.

Botero, G. (2017/1589). *The Reason of State*. Edited by R. Bireley. Cambridge University Press.

Bovens, M. (2003). *De Digitale Republiek: Democratie en rechtsstaat in de informatiemaatschappij*. Amsterdam University Press.

Bovens, M. (2010). Two concepts of accountability: Accountability as a virtue and as a mechanism. *West European Politics* 33, 956–958.

Brennan, G. & Pettit, P. (1990). Unveiling the vote. *British Journal of Political Science* 20(3), 311–333.

Brin, D. (1998). *The Transparent Society: Will Privacy Force Us to Choose Between Privacy and Freedom?* Perseus.

Bruno, J. (2019). Secrecy and Transparency as Fiduciary Duties. Unpublished manuscript.

Buzan, B., Wæver, O., & de Wilde, J. (1998). *Security: A New Framework for Analysis*. Lynne Rienner Publishers.

Caparini, M. (2007). Controlling and overseeing intelligence services in democratic states. In H. Born & M. Caparini (Eds.), *Democratic Control of Intelligence Services: Containing Rogue Elephants*. Ashgate, 3–24.

Chambers, S. (2004). Behind closed doors: Publicity, secrecy, and the quality of deliberation. *Journal of Political Philosophy* 12(4), 398–410.

Chambers, S. & Warren, M. (2023). Why deliberation and voting belong together. *Res Publica* (forthcoming).

Christiano, T. (1996). *The Rule of the Many: Fundamental Issues in Democratic Theory*. Westview Press.

Christiano, T. (2008). *The Constitution of Equality. Democratic Authority and Its Limits*. Oxford University Press.

Clinger, J. (2017). The Kantian publicity principle and the transparency presumption. *Public Integrity* 19(4), 394–403.

Cohen, J. (1997). Deliberation and democratic legitimacy. In J. Bohman & W. Rehg (Eds.), *Deliberative Democracy: Essays on Reason and Politics*. MIT Press, 67–91.

Cohen, J. (2006). Is there a human right to democracy? In C. Sypnowich (Ed.), *The Egalitarian Conscience: Essays in Honour of G.A. Cohen*. Oxford University Press.

Colaresi, M. (2014). *Democracy Declassified: The Secrecy Dilemma in National Security*. Oxford University Press.

Criddle, E., Fox-Decent, E., Gold, A., Kim, S., & Miller, P. (Eds.). (2018). *Fiduciary Government*. Cambridge University Press.

Cross, H. (1953). *The People's Right to Know*. Columbia University Press.

Cucciniello, M., Porumbescu, G.A., & Grimmelikhuijsen, S. (2017). 25 years of transparency research: Evidence and future directions. *Public Administration Review* 77(1), 32–44.

Curtin, D. (2011). *Top Secret Europe*. Inaugural Lecture University of Amsterdam, Amsterdam, the Netherlands.

Da Silveira, P. (2003). Representation, secrecy, and accountability. *Journal of Information Ethics* 12(1), 8–20.

Davis, J. (1998). Access to and transmission of information: Position of the media. In V. Deckmyn & I. Thomson (Eds.), *Openness and Transparency in the European Union*. European Institute of Public Administration, 121–126.

Davis, K. (1991). Kantian "publicity" and political justice. *History of Philosophy Quarterly* 8(4), 409–421.

Davis, S. (2006). Privacy, rights, and moral value. *University of Ottawa law and Technology Journal* 3(1), 111–131.

Davis Cross, M. (2018). Secrecy and the making of CFSP. *West European Politics* 41(4), 914–932.

DeCew, J. (1997). *In Pursuit of Privacy: Law, Ethics, and the Rise of Technology*. Cornell University Press.

de Fine Licht, J. (2013), Do we really want to know? The potentially negative effect of transparency in decision making on perceived legitimacy. *Scandinavian Political Studies* 34, 183–201.

De Fine Licht, J. (2020). The Janus face of transparency: Balancing openness and secrecy in democratic decision-making. In D. Mokrosinska (Ed.), *Transparency and Secrecy in European Democracies: Contested Trade-Offs*. Routledge, 17–35.

Dijstelbloem, H. & Pelizza, A. (2019). The state is the secret: For a relational approach to secrecy. In M. de Goede, E. Bosma, & P. Pallister-Wilkins (Eds.), *Secrecy and Methodology in Critical Security Research*. Routledge, 48–62.

Domscheit-Berg, D. (2011). *Inside WikiLeaks*. Crown Books.

Dowding, K. & van Hees, M. (2008). In praise of manipulation. *British Journal of Political Science* 38: 1–15.

Dryzek, J. (2000). *Deliberative Democracy and Beyond: Liberals, Critics, Contestations*. Oxford University Press.

Dryzek, J. & List, Ch. (2003). Social choice and deliberative democracy: A reconciliation. *British Journal of Political Science* 33(1), 1–28.

Dumsday, T. (2008). Group privacy and government surveillance of religious services. *The Monist* 91(1), 170–186.

Dworkin, R. (1984). Rights as trumps. In J. Waldron (Ed.), *Theories of Rights*. Oxford University Press, 153–167.

Dyzenhaus, D. (2001). Hobbes and the legitimacy of law. *Law and Philosophy* 20, 461–498.

Dyzenhaus, D. (2012). States of emergency. In M. Rosenfeld & A. Sajó (Eds.), *The Oxford Handbook of Comparative Constitutional Law*. Oxford University Press.

Elster, J. (1995). Strategic uses of argument. In K. Arrow et al. (Eds.), *Barriers to Conflict Resolution*. Norton, 237–257.
Elster, J. (1997). The market and the forum: Three varieties of political theory. In J. Bohman & W. Rehg (Eds.), *Deliberative Democracy*. MIT Press, 3–33.
Elster, J. (1998). Deliberation and constitution making. In J. Elster (Ed.), *Deliberative Democracy*. Cambridge University Press, 97–122.
Elster, J. (2013). *Securities against Misrule: Juries, Assemblies and Elections*. Cambridge University Press.
Elster, J. (2015). *Secrecy and Publicity in Votes and Debates*. Cambridge University Press.
Emerson, T. (1976). Legal foundations of the right to know. *Washington University Law Quarterly* 1(1), 1–24.
Engelen, B. & Nys, T. (2013). Against the secret ballot: Toward a new proposal for open voting. *Acta Politica* 48(4), 490–507.
Erkkilä, T. (2020). Transparency in public administration. In W. R. Thompson (Ed.), *Oxford Research Encyclopedia of Politics*. Oxford University Press.
Estlund, D. (2007). *Democratic Authority. A Philosophical Framework*. Princeton University Press.
Fabre, C. (2022). *Spying Through a Glass Darkly: The Ethics of Espionage and Counter-Intelligence*. Oxford University Press.
Fatovic, C. & Kleinerman, B. (2013). *Extra-Legal Power and Legitimacy: Perspectives on Prerogative*. Cambridge University Press.
Feldman, L. (2008). Judging Necessity. Democracy and Extra-legalism. *Political Theory* 36(4), 550–577.
Fenster, M. (2006). The opacity of transparency. *Iowa Law Review* 91, 885–949.
Fenster, M. (2010). Seeing the state: Transparency as metaphor. *Administrative Law Review* 62, 617–672.
Fenster, M. (2015). Transparency in search of a theory. *European Journal of Social Theory* 18(2), 150–167.
Fenster, M. (2017). *The Transparency Fix: Secrets, Leaks, and Uncontrollable Government Information*. Stanford University Press.
Fenster, M. (2021), Bullets of truth: Julian Assange and the politics of transparency. In S. Berger, S. Fengler, D. Owetschkin, & J. Sittmann (Eds.), *Cultures of Transparency: Between Promise and Peril*. Routledge.
Ferejohn, J. (2007). Conversability and deliberation. In G. Brennan, R. Goodin, F. Jackson, & M. Smith (Eds.), *Common Minds: Themes from the Philosophy of Philip Pettit*. Clarendon Press, 121–142.
Ferejohn, J. (2012). Legislation, planning, and deliberation. In H. Landemore & J. Elster (Eds.), *Collective Wisdom: Principles and Mechanisms*. Cambridge University Press, 95–117.
Ferejohn, J. & Pasquino, P. (2004). The law of the exception: A typology of emergency powers. *International Journal of Constitutional Law* 2(2), 210–239.
Fishkin, J.S. (2018). *Democracy When the People Are Thinking: Revitalizing Our Politics through Public Deliberation*. Oxford University Press.
Floridi, L. (2017). Group privacy: A defence and an interpretation. In L. Taylor, L. Floridi, & B. Van der Sloot (Eds.), *Group Privacy: New Challenges of Data Technologies*. Springer, 83–100.

Flowers, A. (2015). *Global Writing for Public Relations. Connecting in English with Stakeholders and Publics Worldwide*. Routledge.

Földes, A. (2016). *Classified Information A Review of Current Legislation across 15 Countries & the EU*. Transparency International. https://ti-defence.org/wp-content/uploads/2016/03/140911-Classified-Information.pdf. Accessed: 7 January 2022.

Frankel, T. (2011). *Fiduciary Law*. Oxford University Press.

Friedrich, C. (1957). *Constitutional Reason of State: The Survival of the Constitutional Order*. Brown University Press.

Fuller, L. (1969). *The Morality of Law*. Yale University Press.

Galoob, S. & Leib, E. (2018). Fiduciary political theory and legitimacy. In E. Criddle, E. Fox-Decent, A. Gold, S. Kim, & P. Miller (Eds.), *Fiduciary Government*. Cambridge University Press, 163–182.

Gasztold, A. (2022). A conspiracy of silence: the CIA black sites in Poland. *International Politics* 59(2), 302–319.

Goodin, R.E. (2008). *Innovating Democracy: Democratic Theory and Practice After the Deliberative Turn*. Oxford University Press.

Gosseries, A. & Parr, T. (2021). Publicity. In E.N. Zalta (Ed.), *The Stanford Encyclopedia of Philosophy*. https://plato.stanford.edu/archives/sum2022/entries/publicity/.

Graham, Ch. (2012). Ministerial Veto on Disclosure of Parts of the Minutes of Cabinet Meetings in March 2003. The Stationery Office.

Green, L. (1988). *The Authority of the State*. Clarendon Press.

Grieve, D. (2012). Exercise of the Executive Order under section 53 of the Freedom of Information Act 2000. www.gov.uk/government/uploads/system/uploads/attachment_data/file/60528/Statement_of_Reasons-31July2012_0.pdf. Accessed: 7 July 2022.

Griffin, J. (2008). *On Human Rights*. Oxford University Press.

Gross, O. (2003). Chaos and rules: Should responses to violent crises always be constitutional? *Yale Law Journal* 112(5): 1012–1134.

Gutmann, A. & Thompson, D. (1996). *Democracy and Disagreement*. Belknap Press.

Gutmann, A. & Thompson, D. 2004. *Why Deliberative Democracy?* Princeton University Press.

Gutmann, A. & Thompson, D. (2012). *The Spirit of Compromise: Why Governing Demands It and Campaigning Undermines It*. Princeton University Press.

Habermas, J. (1996). *Between Facts and Norms: Contributions to a Discourse Theory of Law and Democracy*. MIT Press.

Hadjimatheou, K. (2017). Neither confirm nor deny: Secrecy and disclosure in undercover policing. *Criminal Justice Ethics* 36(3), 279–296.

Hafner-Burton, E. (2008). Sticks and stones: Naming and shaming the human rights enforcement problem. *International Organization* 62(4), 689–716.

Harel, A. (2005). Theories of rights. In M. Golding & W. Edmundson (Eds.), *Blackwell's Guide to the Philosophy of Law and Legal Theory*. Blackwell Publishing, 191–206.

Harel, A. & Sharon, A. (2008). What is really wrong with torture? *Journal of International Criminal Justice* 6(2), 241–259.

Harel, A. & Sharon, A. (2011). Necessity knows no law: On extreme cases and uncodifiable necessities. *The University of Toronto Law Journal* 61(4), 845–865.

Hart, H.L.A. (1982). *Essays on Bentham: Studies in Jurisprudence and Political Theory*. Clarendon Press.

Hart, H.L.A. (1997). *The Concept of Law*. Clarendon Press.

Henkin, L. (1971). The right to know and the duty to withhold: The case of the pentagon papers. *University of Pennsylvania Law Review* 120(2), 271–280.

Hobbes, T. (2003). *Leviathan*. Cambridge University Press.

Hood, C. & Heald, D. (2006). *Transparency: The Key to Better Governance?* Oxford University Press.

Horn, E. (2011). Logics of political secrecy. *Theory, Culture and Society* 28(7–8), 103–122.

Johnson, J. & Orr, S. (2020). *Should Secret Voting Be Mandatory?* Polity Press.

Kagan, S. (1988). *Normative Ethics*. Westview Press.

Kaminski, J.P. (2005). *Secrecy and the Constitutional Convention*. Madison: Center for the Study of the American Constitution.

Kant, I. (1957/1795). Perpetual peace. in L. White Beck, ed., *Kant: On History*. Indianapolis: Bobbs-Merrill, 85–135.

Kant, I. (1996). On a supposed right to lie from philanthropy. In M. Gregor (Ed.), *Practical Philosophy*. Cambridge University Press, 605–616.

Kitrosser, H. (2008). Congressional oversight of national security activity: Improving information funnels. *Cardozo Law Review* 29(3), 1049–1090.

Klosko, G. (2011). Are political obligations content independent? *Political Theory* 39(4), 498–523.

Kogelmann, B. (2021). *Secret Government: The Pathologies of Publicity*. Cambridge University Press.

Kornhauser, L.A. & Sager, L.G. (1986). Unpacking the court. *Yale Law Journal* 96, 82–117.

Kosack, S. & Fung, A. (2014). Does transparency improve governance? *Annual Review of Political Science* 17, 65–87.

Kutz, Ch. (2009). Secret law and the value of publicity. *Ratio Juris* 22(2), 197–217.

Lau, SH.P. & Mui, VL. (2008). Using turn taking to mitigate coordination and conflict problems in the repeated battle of the sexes game. *Theory and Decision* 65(2), 153–183.

Lawford-Smith, H. (2019). *Not in their Name: Are Citizens Culpable for Their States' Actions?* Oxford University Press.

Lee, F. (2019, May 10). *Congressional Transparency: A Word of Caution*. Testimony before the Select Committee on the Modernization of Congress United States House of Representatives.

Lefkowitz, D. (2005). A contractualist defense of democratic authority. *Ratio Juris* 18(3), 346–364.

Lever, A. (2007). Mill and the secret ballot: Beyond coercion and corruption. *Utilitas* 19(3), 354–378.

Levi, M., Sacks, A., & Tyler, T. (2009). Conceptualizing legitimacy, measuring legitimating beliefs. *American Behavioral Scientist* 53(3), 354–375.

Lewis, D.K. (1969). *Convention: A Philosophical Study*. Harvard University Press.

Ligabo, A., Duve, F., & Bertoni, E. (2003). Joint declaration. In *International Mechanisms for Promoting Freedom of Expression*. Organisation for Security and Co-operation in Europe.

List, Ch. (2006). The discursive dilemma and public reason. *Ethics* 116(2), 362–402.

List, Ch. & Puppe, C. (2009). Judgment aggregation: A survey. In P. Anand, P. Pattanaik, & C. Puppe (Eds.), *The handbook of rational and social choice*. Oxford University Press, 457–482.

Locke, J. (1689/1988). *Two Treatises of Government*. Cambridge University Press.

Loi, M. & Christen, M. (2020). Two concepts of group privacy. *Philosophy and Technology* 33, 207–224.

Luban, D. (1996). The principle of publicity. In R. Goodin (Ed.), *The Theory of Institutional Design*. Cambridge University Press, 154–198.

Machiavelli, N. (1988/1532). *The Prince*. Edited by Q. Skinner and R. Price. Cambridge University Press.

Mansbridge, J. (2003). Rethinking representation. *American Political Science Review* 97, 515–528.

Mansbridge, J. (2009). A 'selection model' of political representation. *Journal of Political Philosophy* 17, 369–389.

Markwick, P. (2003). Independent of Content. *Legal Theory* 9(1), 43–61.

Meijer, A. (2013). Understanding the complex dynamics of transparency. *Public Administration Review* 73, 429–439.

Meijer, A., 't Hart, P., & Worthy, B. (2018). Assessing government transparency: An interpretive framework. *Administration & Society* 50(4), 501–526.

Meinecke, F. (1998). *Machiavellism: The Doctrine of Raison d'État in Modern History*. Trans. D. Scott. Transaction Publishers.

Mendelberg, T. (2002). The deliberative citizen: Theory and evidence. In M.X. Delli Carpini, L. Huddy, & R. Shapiro (Eds.), *Research in Micropolitics: Political Decision-Making, Deliberation and Participation*. JAI Press, 151–193.

MOJ (2012). Ministerial veto on disclosure of Cabinet meeting minutes. https://www.gov.uk/government/publications/ministerial-veto-on-disclosure-of-cabinet-meeting-minutes.

Mill, J.S. (1962). *Considerations on Representative Government*. Gateway.

Mokrosinska, D. (2012). *Rethinking Political Obligation: Moral Principles, Communal Ties, Citizenship*. Palgrave Macmillan.

Mokrosinska, D. (2018). The people's right to know and state secrecy. *Canadian Journal of Law & Jurisprudence* 31(1), 87–106.

Mokrosinska, D. (2019). Democratic authority and state secrecy. *Public Affairs Quarterly* 33(1), 1–20.

Mokrosinska, D. (2020a). Why states have no right to privacy, but may be entitled to secrecy: A non-consequentialist defense of state secrecy. *Critical Review of International Social and Political Philosophy* 23(4), 415–444.

Mokrosinska, D. (Ed.). (2020b) *Contested Trade-Offs: Transparency and Secrecy in European Democracies*. Routledge.

Mokrosinska, D. (2022). Necessary but illegitimate: On democracy's secrets. *The Review of Politics* 85(1), 73–97.

Moore, A. & O'Doherty, K. (2014). Deliberative voting. *Journal of Political Philosophy* 22(3), 302–319.

Murray, A. (2005). Should states have a right to informational privacy? In M. Klang & A.D. Murray (Eds.), *Human Rights in the Digital Age*. Glasshouse.

Murray, A. (2011). Transparency, scrutiny and responsiveness: Fashioning a private space within the information society. *The Political Quarterly* 82(4), 509–514.

Narveson, J. (1991). Collective rights? *The Canadian Journal of Law and Jurisprudence* 4(2), 329–345.

Naurin, D. (2006). Transparency, publicity, accountability – the missing links. *Swiss Political Science Review* 12(3), 90–98.

Neocleus, M. (2000). Against security. *Radical Philosophy* 100.

Novak, S. (2023). Off paper: Democracy and the transparency dilemma in EU institutions. In P. Leino-Sandberg, M.Z. Hillebrandt, & I. Koivisto (Eds.), *(In)visible European Government: Critical Approaches to Transparency as an Ideal and a Practice*. Routledge.

Obama, B. (2011). *Memorandum on Transparency and Open Government*. White House. www.archives.gov/files/cui/documents/2009-WH-memo-on-transparency-and-open-government.pdf

O'Flynn, I. & Setälä, M. (2020). Deliberative disagreement and compromise. *Critical Review of International Social and Political Philosophy* 47(1), 1–21.

O'Neill, O. (2002). *A Question of Trust: The BBC Reith Lectures 2002*. Cambridge University Press.

Ottonelli, V. (2010). What does the discursive paradox really mean for democracy? *Political Studies* 58(4), 666–687.

Owen, D. (2020). Power, justification and vindication. In R. Forst (Ed.), *Toleration, Power and the Right to Justification: Rainer Forst in Dialogue*. Manchester University Press.

Parisi, F. & Ghey, N. (2003). The role of reciprocity in international law. *Cornell International Law Journal* 36, 93–123.

Pasternak, A. (2010). Sharing the costs of political injustices. *Politics. Philosophy and Economics* 10, 573–584.

Peled, R. & Rabin, Y. (2011). The constitutional right to information. *Columbia Human Rights Law Review* 42(2), 357–401.

PEN American Center. (2015). *Secret Sources: Whistleblowers, National Security, and Free Expression.*

Pettit, P. (2001). Deliberative democracy and the discursive dilemma. *Philosophical Issues* 11, 268–299.

Pettit, P. (2007). Responsibility incorporated. *Ethics* 117, 171–201.

Pettit, P. & Schweikard, D. (2006). Joint actions and group agents. *Philosophy of Social Sciences* 36(1), 18–39.

Pitkin, H. (1967). *The Concept of Representation*. University of California Press.

Plotke, D. (1997). Representation is democracy. *Constellations* 4(1), 19–34.

Poole, T. (2016). The law of emergency and reason of state. In E. Criddle (Ed.), *Human Rights in Emergencies*. Cambridge University Press.

Posner, E. & Vermeule, A. (2010). *The Executive Unbound: After the Madisonian Republic*. Oxford University Press.

Pozen, D. (2010). Deep secrecy. *Stanford Law Review* 62(2), 257–339.

Przeworski, A., Manin, B., & Stokes, S. (1999). *Democracy, Accountability, and Representation*. Cambridge University Press.

Rawls, J. (1999). *The Law of Peoples*. Harvard University Press.

Raz, J. (1979). *The Authority of Law*. Clarendon Press.

Raz, J. (1986). *The Morality of Freedom*. Clarendon Press.

Raz, J. (1995). *Ethics in the Public Domain: Essays in the Morality of Law and Politics*. Clarendon Press.

Raz, J. (2010). Human rights in the emerging world order. *Transnational Legal Theory* 1, 31–47.

Riese, D. (2020). Secrecy and the preservation of the democratic state: The concept of raison d'état in the German Bundestag. In D. Mokrosinska (Ed.), *Transparency and Secrecy in European Democracies: Contested Trade-offs*. Routledge.

Ripstein, A. (2004). Authority and coercion. *Philosophy and Public Affairs* 32(1), 2–35.

Ritchie, K. (2015). The metaphysics of social groups. *Philosophy Compass* 10, 310–321.

Rittberger, B. & Goetz, K. (2018). Secrecy in Europe. *West European Politics* 41(4): 1–21.

Roberts, A. (2006a). Dashed expectations: Governmental adaptation to transparency rules. In D. Heald & C. Hood (Eds.), *Transparency, the Key to Better Governance?* Oxford University Press.

Roberts, A. (2006b). *Blacked Out: Government Secrecy in the Information Age*. Cambridge University Press.

Roberts, A. (2012). WikiLeaks: the illusion of transparency. *International Review of Administrative Sciences* 78(1), 116–133.

Rolf, J. (2014). The state of nature analogy in international relations theory. *International Relations* 28(2), 159–182.

Rosanvallon, P. (2008). *Counter-Democracy: Politics in an Age of Distrust*. Cambridge University Press.

Rosenblum, N. (2005). Constitutional reason of state: The fear factor. In A. Sarat (Ed.), *Dissent in Dangerous Times*. University of Michigan Press.

Sagar, R. (2007). On combating the abuse of state secrecy. *Journal of Political Philosophy* 15(4), 404–427.

Sagar, R. (2013). *Secrets and Leaks: The Dilemma of State Secrecy*. Princeton University Press.

Schauer, F. (1983). Rights and the right to know. *Philosophic Exchange* 14, 65–76.

Scheffler, S. (Ed.). (1988). *Consequentialism and Its Critics*. Oxford University Press.

Schelling, T. (1960). *The Strategy of Conflict*. Harvard University Press.

Scheppele, K.L. (2006). We are all post-9/11 now. *Fordham Law Review* 75(2), 607–629.

Scheuerman, W. (2006). Emergency powers and the rule of law after 9/11. *Journal of Political Philosophy* 14(1), 61–84.

Schmitt, C. (2014). *Dictatorship. From the Origin of the Modern Concept of Sovereignty to Proletarian Class Struggle*. Translated by M. Hoelzl and G. Ward Polity Press.

Schmitt, C. (2005). *Political Theology*. Chicago University Press.

Schoenfeld, G. (2010). *Necessary Secrets, National Security, The Media, and The Rule of Law*. Norton & Co.

Seidman, L. (2005). Torture's truth. *University of Chicago Law Review* 72(3), 881–918.

Serota, K. & O'Doherty, K. (2022). The discursive functions of deliberative voting. *Journal of Deliberative Democracy* 18(1), 1–12.

Snowe, O.J. (2013). The effect of modern partisanship on legislative effectiveness in the 112th Congress. *Harvard Journal on Legislation* 50(1), 21–40.

Soper, P. (1989). Legal theory and the claim of authority. *Philosophy and Public Affairs* 18(3), 209–239.

Stiglitz, J. (2002). Transparency in government. In World Bank Institute (Ed.), *The Right to Tell: The Role of Mass Media in Economic Development*. The World Bank, 27–44.

Sumner, L.W. (1987). *The Moral Foundation of Rights*. Clarendon Press.

The White House. 2009. *Transparency and Open Government. Memorandum For the Heads of Executive Departments and Agencies*. https://www.govinfo.gov/content/pkg/DCPD-200900010/pdf/DCPD-200900010.pdf.

Thomas, O. (2020). Paradoxical secrecy in British freedom of information law. In D. Mokrosinska (Ed.), *Contested Trade-Offs: Transparency and Secrecy in European Democracies*. Routledge.

Thompson, D. (1987). *Political Ethics and Public Office*. Harvard University Press.

Thompson, D. (1999). Democratic secrecy: The dilemma of accountability. *Political Science Quarterly* 114(2), 181–193.

Thompson, D. (2008). Deliberative democratic theory and empirical research. *Annual Review of Political Science* 11(1), 497–520.

Tushnet, M. (2005). Emergencies and the idea of constitutionalism. In M. Tushnet (Ed.), *The Constitution in Wartime: Beyond Alarmism and Complacency*. Duke University Press.

Ulbert, C. & Risse, T. (2005). Deliberately changing the discourse: What does make arguing effective? *Acta Politica* 40, 351–367.

Urbinati, N. (2006). *Representative Democracy. Principles and Genealogy*. Chicago University Press.

Valentini, L. (2018). The content-independence of political obligation: What it is and how to test it. *Legal Theory* 24(2), 135–157.

Vermeule, A. (2015). Open-secret voting. In J. Elster (Ed.), *Secrecy and Publicity in Votes and Debates*. Cambridge University Press, 215–229.

Viehoff, D. (2014). Democratic equality and political authority. *Philosophy and Public Affairs* 42(4), 337–375.

Waldron, J. (2005). Torture and positive law: Jurisprudence for the White House. *Columbia Law Review* 105(6).

Waldron, J. (2016). *Political Political Theory: Essays on Institutions*. Harvard University Press.

Wang, Q. & Guan, Z. (2022). Can sunlight disperse mistrust? A meta-analysis of the effect of transparency on citizens' trust in government. *Journal of Public Administration Research and Theory*, 1–15.

Warren, M. & Mansbridge, J. (2016). Deliberative negotiation. In J. Mansbridge & C. Martin (Eds.), *Political Negotiation: A Handbook*. Brookings Institution Press, 141–196.

Wendt, F. (2019). *Authority*. Polity.

Westin, A. (1967). *Privacy and Freedom*. Atheneum.

Williams, H. (1983). *Kant's Political Philosophy*. Basil Blackwell.

Worthy, B. (2010). More open but not more trusted? The effect of the Freedom of Information Act 2000 on the United Kingdom central government. *Governance* 23(4), 561–582.

Worthy, B. (2020). Freedom of information in Europe: Creation, context and conflict. In D. Mokrosinska (Ed.), *Contested Trade-Offs: Transparency and Secrecy in European Democracies*. Routledge.

Index

Note: Page numbers in **bold** indicate a table on the corresponding page.

For Product Safety Concerns and Information please contact our EU representative GPSR@taylorandfrancis.com
Taylor & Francis Verlag GmbH, Kaufingerstraße 24, 80331 München, Germany

www.ingramcontent.com/pod-product-compliance
Ingram Content Group UK Ltd.
Pitfield, Milton Keynes, MK11 3LW, UK
UKHW020939200926
475569UK00012B/36
* 9 7 8 0 3 6 7 5 3 9 2 3 8 *